RESUMES FOR

COMMUNICATIONS CAREERS

VGM Professional Resumes Series

THIRD EDITION

RESUMES FOR

COMMUNCATIONS CAREERS

With Sample Cover Letters

The Editors of VGM Career Books

VGM Career Books
Chicago New York San Francisco Lisbon London Madrid Mexico City
Milan New Delhi San Juan Seoul Singapore Sydney Toronto

Library of Congress Cataloging-in-Publication Data

> Resumes for communications careers / the editors of VGM Career Books.—
3rd ed.
>
>> p.   cm. — (VGM professional resumes series)
>
> ISBN 0-07-140593-3
> 1. Communication—Vocational guidance.   2. Resumes (Employment)
I. VGM Career Horizons (Firm).   II. Series.

P91.6 .R4   2003
302.2'023—dc21   2002028079

1 2 3 4 5 6 7 8 9 0   QPD/QPD   2 1 0 9 8 7 6 5 4 3

ISBN 0-07-140593-3

McGraw-Hill books are available at special quantity discounts to use as premiums and sales promotions, or for use in corporate training programs. For more information, please write to the Director of Special Sales, Professional Publishing, McGraw-Hill, Two Penn Plaza, New York, NY 10121-2298. Or contact your local bookstore.

This book is printed on acid-free paper.

Contents

Introduction

Your resume is a piece of paper (or an electronic document) that serves to introduce you to the people who will eventually hire you. To write a thoughtful resume, you must thoroughly assess your personality, your accomplishments, and the skills you have acquired. The act of composing and submitting a resume also requires you to carefully consider the company or individual that might hire you. What are they looking for, and how can you meet their needs? This book shows you how to organize your personal information and experience into a concise and well-written resume, so that your qualifications and potential as an employee will be understood easily and quickly by a complete stranger.

Writing the resume is just one step in what can be a daunting job-search process, but it is an important element in the chain of events that will lead you to your new position. While you are probably a talented, bright, and charming person, your resume may not reflect these qualities. A poorly written resume can get you nowhere; a well-written resume can land you an interview and potentially a job. A good resume can even lead the interviewer to ask you questions that will allow you to talk about your strengths and highlight the skills you can bring to a prospective employer. Even a person with very little experience can find a good job if he or she is assisted by a thoughtful and polished resume.

Lengthy, typewritten resumes are a thing of the past. Today, employers do not have the time or the patience for verbose documents; they look for tightly composed, straightforward, action-based resumes. Although a one-page resume is the norm, a two-page resume may be warranted if you have had extensive job experience or have changed careers and truly need the space to properly position yourself. If, after careful editing, you still need more than one page to present yourself, it's acceptable to use a second page. A crowded resume that's hard to read would be the worst of your choices.

Distilling your work experience, education, and interests into such a small space requires preparation and thought. This book takes you step-by-step through the process of crafting an effective resume that will stand out in today's competitive marketplace. It serves as a workbook and a place to write down your experiences, while also including the techniques you'll need to pull all the necessary elements together. In the following pages, you'll find many examples of resumes that are specific to your area of interest. Study them for inspiration and find what appeals to you. There are a variety of ways to organize and present your information; inside, you'll find several that will be suitable to your needs. Good luck landing the job of your dreams!

RESUMES FOR
COMMUNICATIONS CAREERS

The Elements of an Effective Resume

An effective resume is composed of information that employers are most interested in knowing about a prospective job applicant. This information is conveyed by a few essential elements. The following is a list of elements that are found in most resumes—some essential, some optional. Later in this chapter, we will further examine the role of each of these elements in the makeup of your resume.

- Heading

- Objective and/or Keyword Section

- Work Experience

- Education

- Honors

- Activities

- Certificates and Licenses

- Publications

- Professional Memberships

- Special Skills

- Personal Information

- References

The first step in preparing your resume is to gather information about yourself and your past accomplishments. Later you will refine this information, rewrite it using effective language, and organize it into an attractive layout. But first, let's take a look at each of these important elements individually so you can judge their appropriateness for your resume.

Heading

Although the heading may seem to be the simplest section of your resume, be careful not to take it lightly. It is the first section your prospective employer will see, and it contains the information she or he will need to contact you. At the very least, the heading must contain your name, your home address, and, of course, a phone number where you can be reached easily.

In today's high-tech world, many of us have multiple ways that we can be contacted. You may list your E-mail address if you are reasonably sure the employer makes use of this form of communication. Keep in mind, however, that others may have access to your E-mail messages if you send them from an account provided by your current company. If this is a concern, do not list your work E-mail address on your resume. If you are able to take calls at your current place of business, you should include your work number, because most employers will attempt to contact you during typical business hours.

If you have voice mail or a reliable answering machine at home or at work, list its number in the heading and make sure your greeting is professional and clear. Always include at least one phone number in your heading, even if it is a temporary number, where a prospective employer can leave a message.

You might have a dozen different ways to be contacted, but you do not need to list all of them. Confine your numbers or addresses to those that are the easiest for the prospective employer to use and the simplest for you to retrieve.

Objective

When seeking a specific career path, it is important to list a job or career objective on your resume. This statement helps employers know the direction you see yourself taking, so they can determine whether your goals are in line with those of their organization and the position available. Normally, an objective is one to two sentences long. Its contents will vary depending on your career field, goals, and personality. The objective can be specific or general, but it should always be to the point. See the sample resumes in this book for examples.

If you are planning to use this resume online, or you suspect your potential employer is likely to scan your resume, you will want to include a "keyword" in the objective. This allows a prospective employer, searching hundreds of resumes for a specific skill or position objective, to locate the keyword and find your resume. In essence, a keyword is what's "hot" in your particular field at a given time. It's a buzzword, a shorthand way of getting a particular message across at a glance. For example, if you are a lawyer, your objective might state your desire to work in the area of corporate litigation. In this case, someone searching for the keyword "corporate litigation" will pull up your resume and know that you want to plan, research, and present cases at trial on behalf of the corporation. If your objective states that you "desire a challenging position in systems design," the keyword is "systems design," an industry-specific, shorthand way of saying that you want to be involved in assessing the need for, acquiring, and implementing high-technology systems. These are keywords and every industry has them, so it's becoming more and more important to include a few in your resume. (You may need to conduct additional research to make sure you know what keywords are most likely to be used in your desired industry, profession, or situation.)

There are many resume and job-search sites online. Like most things in the online world, they vary a great deal in quality. Use your discretion. If you plan to apply for jobs online or advertise your availability this way, you will want to design a scannable resume. This type of resume uses a format that can be easily scanned into a computer and added to a database. Scanning allows a prospective employer to use keywords to quickly review each applicant's experience and skills, and (in the event that there are many candidates for the job) to keep your resume for future reference.

Many people find that it is worthwhile to create two or more versions of their basic resume. You may want an intricately designed resume on high-quality paper to mail or hand out *and* a resume that is designed to be scanned into a computer and saved on a database or an online job site. You can even create a resume in ASCII text to E-mail to prospective employers. For further information, you may wish to refer to the *Guide to Internet Job Searching*, by Frances Roehm and Margaret Dikel, updated and published every other year by VGM Career Books, a division of the McGraw-Hill Companies. This excellent book contains helpful and detailed information about formatting a resume for Internet use. To get you started, in Chapter 3 we have included a list of things to keep in mind when creating electronic resumes.

Although it is usually a good idea to include an objective, in some cases this element is not necessary. The goal of the objective statement is to provide the employer with an idea of where you see yourself going in the field. However, if you are uncertain of the exact nature of the job you seek, including an objective that is too specific could result in your not being considered for a host of perfectly acceptable positions. If you decide not to use an objective heading in your resume, you should definitely incorporate the information that would be conveyed in the objective into your cover letter.

Work Experience

Work experience is arguably the most important element of them all. Unless you are a recent graduate or former homemaker with little or no relevant work experience, your current and former positions will provide the central focus of the resume. You will want this section to be as complete and carefully constructed as possible. By thoroughly examining your work experience, you can get to the heart of your accomplishments and present them in a way that demonstrates and highlights your qualifications.

If you are just entering the workforce, your resume will probably focus on your education, but you should also include information on your work or volunteer experiences. Although you will have less information about work experience than a person who has held multiple positions or is advanced in his or her career, the amount of information is not what is most important in this section. How the information is presented and what it says about you as a worker and a person is what really counts.

As you create this section of your resume, remember the need for accuracy. Include all the necessary information about each of your jobs, including your job title, dates of employment, name of your employer, city, state, responsibilities, special projects you handled, and accomplishments. Be sure to list only accomplishments for which you were directly responsible. And don't be alarmed if you haven't participated in or worked on special projects, because this section may not be relevant to certain jobs.

The most common way to list your work experience is in *reverse chronological order*. In other words, start with your most recent job and work your way backward. This way, your prospective employer sees your current (and often most important) position before considering your past employment. Your most recent position, if it's the most important in terms of responsibilities and relevance to the job for which you are applying, should also be the one that includes the most information as compared to your previous positions.

Even if the work itself seems unrelated to your proposed career path, you should list any job or experience that will help "sell" your talents. If you were promoted or given greater responsibilities or commendations, be sure to mention the fact.

The following worksheet is provided to help you organize your experiences in the working world. It will also serve as an excellent resource to refer to when updating your resume in the future.

WORK EXPERIENCE

Job One:

Job Title _____

Dates _____

Employer _____

City, State _____

Major Duties _____

_____

_____

_____

_____

_____

_____

_____

_____

Special Projects _____

_____

_____

_____

Accomplishments _____

_____

_____

_____

_____

_____

Job Two:

Job Title _____

Dates _____

Employer _____

City, State _____

Major Duties _____

_____

_____

_____

_____

_____

_____

_____

Special Projects _____

_____

_____

_____

Accomplishments _____

_____

_____

_____

_____

_____

_____

_____

Job Three:

Job Title _____

Dates _____

Employer _____

City, State _____

Major Duties _____

_____

_____

_____

_____

_____

_____

_____

Special Projects _____

_____

_____

_____

Accomplishments _____

_____

_____

_____

_____

_____

_____

_____

Job Four:

Job Title _____

Dates _____

Employer _____

City, State _____

Major Duties _____

_____

_____

_____

_____

_____

_____

_____

_____

Special Projects _____

_____

_____

_____

Accomplishments _____

_____

_____

_____

_____

_____

_____

_____

Education

Education is usually the second most important element of a resume. Your educational background is often a deciding factor in an employer's decision to interview you. Highlight your accomplishments in school as much as you did those accomplishments at work. If you are looking for your first professional job, your education or life experience will be your greatest assets because your related work experience will be minimal. In this case, the education section becomes the most important means of selling yourself.

Include in this section all the degrees or certificates you have received; your major or area of concentration; all of the honors you earned; and any relevant activities you participated in, organized, or chaired. Again, list your most recent schooling first. If you have completed graduate-level work, begin with that and work your way back through your undergraduate education. If you have completed college, you generally should not list your high school experience; do so only if you earned special honors, you had a grade point average that was much better than the norm, or this was your highest level of education.

If you have completed a large number of credit hours in a subject that may be relevant to the position you are seeking but did not obtain a degree, you may wish to list the hours or classes you completed. Keep in mind, however, that you may be asked to explain why you did not finish the program. If you are currently in school, list the degree, certificate, or license you expect to obtain and the projected date of completion.

The following worksheet will help you gather the information you need for this section of your resume.

EDUCATION

School One _____

Major or Area of Concentration _____

Degree _____

Dates _____

School Two _____

Major or Area of Concentration _____

Degree _____

Dates _____

Honors

If you include an honors section in your resume, you should highlight any awards, honors, or memberships in honorary societies that you have received. (You may also incorporate this information into your education section.) Often, the honors are academic in nature, but this section also may be used for special achievements in sports, clubs, or other school activities. Always include the name of the organization awarding the honor and the date(s) received. Use the following worksheet to help you gather your information.

HONORS

Honor One _____

Awarding Organization _____

Date(s) _____

Honor Two _____

Awarding Organization _____

Date(s) _____

Honor Three _____

Awarding Organization _____

Date(s) _____

Honor Four _____

Awarding Organization _____

Date(s) _____

Honor Five _____

Awarding Organization _____

Date(s) _____

Activities

Perhaps you have been active in different organizations or clubs; often an employer will look at such involvement as evidence of initiative, dedication, and good social skills. Examples of your ability to take a leading role in a group should be included on a resume, if you can provide them. The activities section of your resume should present neighborhood and community activities, volunteer positions, and so forth. In general, you may want to avoid listing any organization whose name indicates the race, creed, sex, age, marital status, sexual orientation, or nation of origin of its members because this could expose you to discrimination. Use the following worksheet to list the specifics of your activities.

ACTIVITIES

Organization/Activity _____

Accomplishments _____

_____

_____

Organization/Activity _____

Accomplishments _____

_____

_____

Organization/Activity _____

Accomplishments _____

_____

_____

As your work experience grows through the years, your school activities and honors will carry less weight and be emphasized less in your resume. Eventually, you will probably list only your degree and any major honors received. As time goes by, your job performance and the experience you've gained become the most important elements in your resume, which should change to reflect this.

Certificates and Licenses

If your chosen career path requires specialized training, you may already have certificates or licenses. You should list these if the job you are seeking requires them and you, of course, have acquired them. If you have applied for a license but have not yet received it, use the phrase "application pending."

License requirements vary by state. If you have moved or are planning to relocate to another state, check with that state's board or licensing agency for all licensing requirements.

Always make sure that all of the information you list is completely accurate. Locate copies of your certificates and licenses, and check the exact date and name of the accrediting agency. Use the following worksheet to organize the necessary information.

CERTIFICATES AND LICENSES

Name of License _____

Licensing Agency _____

Date Issued _____

Name of License _____

Licensing Agency _____

Date Issued _____

Name of License _____

Licensing Agency _____

Date Issued _____

Publications

Some professions strongly encourage or even require that you publish. If you have written, coauthored, or edited any books, articles, professional papers, or works of a similar nature that pertain to your field, you will definitely want to include this element. Remember to list the date of publication and the publisher's name, and specify whether you were the sole author or a coauthor. Book, magazine, or journal titles are generally italicized, while the titles of articles within a larger publication appear in quotes. (Check with your reference librarian for more about the appropriate way to present this information.) For scientific or research papers, you will need to give the date, place, and audience to whom the paper was presented.

Use the following worksheet to help you gather the necessary information about your publications.

PUBLICATIONS

Title and Type (Note, Article, etc.) _____

Title of Publication (Journal, Book, etc.) _____

Publisher _____

Date Published _____

Title and Type (Note, Article, etc.) _____

Title of Publication (Journal, Book, etc.) _____

Publisher _____

Date Published _____

Title and Type (Note, Article, etc.) _____

Title of Publication (Journal, Book, etc.) _____

Publisher _____

Date Published _____

Professional Memberships

Another potential element in your resume is a section listing professional memberships. Use this section to describe your involvement in professional associations, unions, and similar organizations. It is to your advantage to list any professional memberships that pertain to the job you are seeking. Many employers see your membership as representative of your desire to stay up-to-date and connected in your field. Include the dates of your involvement and whether you took part in any special activities or held any offices within the organization. Use the following worksheet to organize your information.

PROFESSIONAL MEMBERSHIPS

Name of Organization _____

Office(s) Held_____

Activities _____

Dates _____

Name of Organization _____

Office(s) Held_____

Activities _____

Dates _____

Name of Organization _____

Office(s) Held_____

Activities _____

Dates _____

Name of Organization _____

Office(s) Held_____

Activities _____

Dates _____

Special Skills

The special skills section of your resume is the place to mention any special abilities you have that relate to the job you are seeking. You can use this element to present certain talents or experiences that are not necessarily a part of your education or work experience. Common examples include fluency in a foreign language, extensive travel abroad, or knowledge of a particular computer application. "Special skills" can encompass a wide range of talents, and this section can be used creatively. However, for each skill you list, you should be able to describe how it would be a direct asset in the type of work you're seeking because employers may ask just that in an interview. If you can't think of a way to do this, it may be extraneous information.

Personal Information

Some people include personal information on their resumes. This is generally not recommended, but you might wish to include it if you think that something in your personal life, such as a hobby or talent, has some bearing on the position you are seeking. This type of information is often referred to at the beginning of an interview, when it may be used as an "icebreaker." Of course, personal information regarding your age, marital status, race, religion, or sexual orientation should never appear on your resume as *personal information*. It should be given only in the context of memberships and activities, and only when doing so would not expose you to discrimination.

References

References are not usually given on the resume itself, but a prospective employer needs to know that you have references who may be contacted if necessary. All you need to include is a single sentence at the end of the resume: "References are available upon request," or even simply, "References available." Have a reference list ready—your interviewer may ask to see it! Contact each person on the list ahead of time to see whether it is all right for you to use him or her as a reference. This way, the person has a chance to think about what to say *before* the call occurs. This helps ensure that you will obtain the best reference possible.

Chapter 2

Writing Your Resume

N ow that you have gathered the information for each section of your resume, it's time to write it out in a way that will get the attention of the reviewer—hopefully, your future employer! The language you use in your resume will affect its success, so you must be careful and conscientious. Translate the facts you have gathered into the active, precise language of resume writing. You will be aiming for a resume that keeps the reader's interest and highlights your accomplishments in a concise and effective way.

Resume writing is unlike any other form of writing. Although your seventh-grade composition teacher would not approve, the rules of punctuation and sentence building are often completely ignored. Instead, you should try for a functional, direct writing style that focuses on the use of verbs and other words that imply action on your part. Writing with action words and strong verbs characterizes you to potential employers as an energetic, active person, someone who completes tasks and achieves results from his or her work. Resumes that do not make use of action words can sound passive and stale. These resumes are not effective and do not get the attention of any employer, no matter how qualified the applicant. Choose words that display your strengths and demonstrate your initiative. The following list of commonly used verbs will help you create a strong resume:

administered	assembled
advised	assumed responsibility
analyzed	billed
arranged	built

carried out	inspected
channeled	interviewed
collected	introduced
communicated	invented
compiled	maintained
completed	managed
conducted	met with
contacted	motivated
contracted	negotiated
coordinated	operated
counseled	orchestrated
created	ordered
cut	organized
designed	oversaw
determined	performed
developed	planned
directed	prepared
dispatched	presented
distributed	produced
documented	programmed
edited	published
established	purchased
expanded	recommended
functioned as	recorded
gathered	reduced
handled	referred
hired	represented
implemented	researched
improved	reviewed

saved	supervised
screened	taught
served as	tested
served on	trained
sold	typed
suggested	wrote

Let's look at two examples that differ only in their writing style. The first resume section is ineffective because it does not use action words to accent the applicant's work experiences.

WORK EXPERIENCE
Regional Sales Manager

Manager of sales representatives from seven states. Manager of twelve food chain accounts in the East. In charge of the sales force's planned selling toward specific goals. Supervisor and trainer of new sales representatives. Consulting for customers in the areas of inventory management and quality control.

Special Projects: Coordinator and sponsor of annual food-industry sales seminar.

Accomplishments: Monthly regional volume went up 25 percent during my tenure while, at the same time, a proper sales/cost ratio was maintained. Customer-company relations were improved.

In the following paragraph, we have rewritten the same section using action words. Notice how the tone has changed. It now sounds stronger and more active. This person accomplished goals and really *did* things.

WORK EXPERIENCE
Regional Sales Manager

Managed sales representatives from seven states. Oversaw twelve food chain accounts in the eastern United States. Directed the sales force in planned selling toward specific goals. Supervised and trained new sales representatives. Counseled customers in the areas of inventory management and quality control. Coordinated and sponsored the annual Food Industry Seminar. Increased monthly regional volume 25 percent and helped to improve customer-company relations during my tenure.

One helpful way to construct the work experience section is to make use of your actual job descriptions—the written duties and expectations your employers had for a person in your current or former position. Job descriptions are rarely written in proper resume language, so you will have to rework them, but they do include much of the information necessary to create this section of your resume. If you have access to job descriptions for your former positions, you can use the details to construct an action-oriented paragraph. Often, your human resources department can provide a job description for your current position.

The following is an example of a typical human resources job description, followed by a rewritten version of the same description employing action words and specific details about the job. Again, pay attention to the style of writing instead of the content, as the details of your own experience will be unique.

WORK EXPERIENCE
Public Administrator I

Responsibilities: Coordinate and direct public services to meet the needs of the nation, state, or community. Analyze problems; work with special committees and public agencies; recommend solutions to governing bodies.

Aptitudes and Skills: Ability to relate to and communicate with people; solve complex problems through analysis; plan, organize, and implement policies and programs. Knowledge of political systems, financial management, personnel administration, program evaluation, and organizational theory.

WORK EXPERIENCE
Public Administrator I

Wrote pamphlets and conducted discussion groups to inform citizens of legislative processes and consumer issues. Organized and supervised 25 interviewers. Trained interviewers in effective communication skills.

After you have written out your resume, you are ready to begin the next important step: assembly and layout.

Chapter 3

Assembly and Layout

A t this point, you've gathered all the necessary information for your resume and rewritten it in language that will impress your potential employers. Your next step is to assemble the sections in a logical order and lay them out on the page neatly and attractively to achieve the desired effect: getting the interview.

Assembly

The order of the elements in a resume makes a difference in its overall effect. Clearly, you would not want to bury your name and address somewhere in the middle of the resume. Nor would you want to lead with a less important section, such as special skills. Put the elements in an order that stresses your most important accomplishments and the things that will be most appealing to your potential employer. For example, if you are new to the workforce, you will want the reviewer to read about your education and life skills before any part-time jobs you may have held for short durations. On the other hand, if you have been gainfully employed for several years and currently hold an important position in your company, you should list your work accomplishments ahead of your educational information, which has become less pertinent with time.

Certain things should always be included in your resume, but others are optional. The following list shows you which are which. You might want to use it as a checklist to be certain that you have included all of the necessary information.

Essential	Optional
Name	Cellular Phone Number
Address	Pager Number
Phone Number	E-Mail Address or Website Address
Work Experience	Voice Mail Number
Education	Job Objective
References Phrase	Honors
	Special Skills
	Publications
	Professional Memberships
	Activities
	Certificates and Licenses
	Personal Information
	Graphics
	Photograph

Your choice of optional sections depends on your own background and employment needs. Always use information that will put you in a favorable light—unless it's absolutely essential, avoid anything that will prompt the interviewer to ask questions about your weaknesses or something else that could be unflattering. Make sure your information is accurate and truthful. If your honors are impressive, include them in the resume. If your activities in school demonstrate talents that are necessary for the job you are seeking, allow space for a section on activities. If you are applying for a position that requires ornamental illustration, you may want to include border illustrations or graphics that demonstrate your talents in this area. If you are answering an advertisement for a job that requires certain physical traits, a photo of yourself might be appropriate. A person applying for a job as a computer programmer would *not* include a photo as part of his or her resume. Each resume is unique, just as each person is unique.

Types of Resumes

So far we have focused on the most common type of resume—the *reverse chronological* resume—in which your most recent job is listed first. This is the type of resume usually preferred by those who have to read a large number of resumes, and it is by far the most popular and widely circulated. However, this style of presentation may not be the most effective way to highlight *your* skills and accomplishments.

For example, if you are reentering the workforce after many years or are trying to change career fields, the *functional* resume may work best. This type of resume puts the focus on your achievements instead of the sequence of your work history. In the functional resume, your experience is presented through your general accomplishments and the skills you have developed in your working life.

A functional resume is assembled from the same information you gathered in Chapter 1. The main difference lies in how you organize the information. Essentially, the work experience section is divided in two, with your job duties and accomplishments constituting one section and your employers' names, cities, and states; your positions; and the dates employed making up the other. Place the first section near the top of your resume, just below your job objective (if used), and call it *Accomplishments* or *Achievements*. The second section, containing the bare essentials of your work history, should come after the accomplishments section and can be called *Employment History*, since it is a chronological overview of your former jobs.

The other sections of your resume remain the same. The work experience section is the only one affected in the functional format. By placing the section that focuses on your achievements at the beginning, you draw attention to these achievements. This puts less emphasis on whom you worked for and when, and more on what you did and what you are capable of doing.

If you are changing careers, the emphasis on skills and achievements is important. The identities of previous employers (who aren't part of your new career field) need to be downplayed. A functional resume can help accomplish this task. If you are reentering the workforce after a long absence, a functional resume is the obvious choice. And if you lack full-time work experience, you will need to draw attention away from this fact and put the focus on your skills and abilities. You may need to highlight your volunteer activities and part-time work. Education may also play a more important role in your resume.

The type of resume that is right for you will depend on your personal circumstances. It may be helpful to create both types and then compare them. Which one presents you in the best light? Examples of both types of resumes are included in this book. Use the sample resumes in Chapter 5 to help you decide on the content, presentation, and look of your own resume.

Special Tips for Electronic Resumes

Because there are many details to consider in writing a resume that will be posted or transmitted on the Internet, or one that will be scanned into a computer when it is received, we suggest that you refer to the *Guide to Internet Job Searching*, by Frances Roehm and Margaret Dikel, as previously mentioned. However, here are some brief, general guidelines to follow if you expect your resume to be scanned into a computer.

- Use standard fonts in which none of the letters touch.

- Keep in mind that underlining, italics, and fancy scripts may not scan well.

- Use boldface and capitalization to set off elements. Again, make sure letters don't touch. Leave at least a quarter inch between lines of type.

- Keep information and elements at the left margin. Centering, columns, and even indenting may change when the resume is optically scanned.

- Do not use any lines, boxes, or graphics.

- Place the most important information at the top of the first page. If you use two pages, put "Page 1 of 2" at the bottom of the first page and put your name and "Page 2 of 2" at the top of the second page.

- List each telephone number on its own line in the header.

- Use multiple keywords or synonyms for what you do to make sure your qualifications will be picked up if a prospective employer is searching for them. Use nouns that are keywords for your profession.

- Be descriptive in your titles. For example, don't just use "assistant"; use "legal office assistant."

- Make sure the contrast between print and paper is good. Use a high-quality laser printer and white or very light colored 8½-by-11-inch paper.

- Mail a high-quality laser print or an excellent copy. Do not fold or use staples, as this might interfere with scanning. You may, however, use paper clips.

In addition to creating a resume that works well for scanning, you may want to have a resume that can be E-mailed to reviewers. Because you may not know what word processing application the recipient uses, the best format to use is ASCII text. (ASCII stands for "American Standard Code for Information Exchange.") It allows people with very different software platforms to exchange and understand information. (E-mail operates on this principle.) ASCII is a simple, text-only language, which means you can include only simple text. There can be no use of boldface, italics, or even paragraph indentations.

To create an ASCII resume, just use your normal word processing program; when finished, save it as a "text only" document. You will find this option under the "save" or "save as" command. Here is a list of things to *avoid* when crafting your electronic resume:

- Tabs. Use your space bar. Tabs will not work.

- Any special characters, such as mathematical symbols.

- Word wrap. Use hard returns (the return key) to make line breaks.

- Centering or other formatting. Align everything at the left margin.

- Bold or italic fonts. Everything will be converted to plain text when you save the file as a "text only" document.

Check carefully for any mistakes before you save the document as a text file. Spellcheck and proofread it several times; then ask someone with a keen eye to go over it again for you. Remember: the key is to keep it simple. Any attempt to make this resume pretty or decorative may result in a resume that is confusing and hard to read. After you have saved the document, you can cut and paste it into an E-mail or onto a website.

Layout for a Paper Resume

A great deal of care—and much more formatting—is necessary to achieve an attractive layout for your paper resume. There is no single appropriate layout that applies to every resume, but there are a few basic rules to follow in putting your resume on paper:

- Leave a comfortable margin on the sides, top, and bottom of the page (usually one to one and a half inches).

- Use appropriate spacing between the sections (two to three line spaces are usually adequate).

- Be consistent in the *type* of headings you use for different sections of your resume. For example, if you capitalize the heading EMPLOY-MENT HISTORY, don't use initial capitals and underlining for a section of equal importance, such as <u>Education</u>.

- Do not use more than one font in your resume. Stay consistent by choosing a font that is fairly standard and easy to read, and don't change it for different sections. Beware of the tendency to try to make your resume original by choosing fancy type styles; your resume may end up looking unprofessional instead of creative. Unless you are in a very creative and artistic field, you should almost always stick with tried-and-true type styles like Times New Roman and Palatino, which are often used in business writing. In the area of resume styles, conservative is usually the best way to go.

- Always try to fit your resume on one page. If you are having trouble with this, you may be trying to say too much. Edit out any repetitive or unnecessary information, and shorten descriptions of earlier jobs where possible. Ask a friend you trust for feedback on what seems unnecessary or unimportant. For example, you may have included too many optional sections. Today, with the prevalence of the personal computer as a tool, there is no excuse for a poorly laid out resume. Experiment with variations until you are pleased with the result.

CHRONOLOGICAL RESUME

Lucas Jackson
2399 S. Division • Grand Rapids, MI 49503
(616) 555-9354
Cell: (616) 555-2819
lucasjackson@xxx.com

Objective

Apply my skills as a content expert to a new challenge with a company focused on quality, dedication, and ingenuity.

Work

1998 to present

Content Strategist, Sonic Consulting, Grand Rapids, MI

Provide digital solutions for clients interested in establishing their presence online. Make recommendations on content assets, third-party content partnerships, and content management systems. Direct copywriters and design teams to fulfill the clients' objectives and create brand strategies.

1996 to 1998

Website Manager, *Crash! Magazine*, Detroit, MI

Directed the online version of *Crash! Magazine* and ensured design and content guidelines of the site followed those of the print version. Coordinated special events to drive traffic to the site resulting in a 75 percent increase in hits over four months. Created and edited content specifically for the site to establish its own identity.

1994 to 1996

Writer, *Digital City Magazine*, Detroit, MI

Researched and wrote articles covering the emerging Internet business and issues that relate to that unique business sector. Interviewed people involved in cutting-edge development on the Web and analyzed the business implications of this unique medium.

Skills

- Intimate familiarity with standard style guides including *AP, Chicago Manual, MLA,* and *Wired.*
- Very knowledgeable in the use and merits of content management systems such as Vignette, ePrise, and BroadVision.
- Uncanny ability to merge creative vision with business objectives to create distinctive and engaging content.

References available upon request

FUNCTIONAL RESUME

Katrina Parker
1402 Greenbriar Road
Charleston, WV 25304
(304) 555-1704

Applications and Systems Programmer

Credentials

- B.S. in Computer Science—March 1995—University of Michigan; minor in Accounting
- Knowledge of COBOL, Fortran, Pascal, C, C Plus, BASIC, CAD/CAM, RPG II, Assembly language #68000, 8086 & 6502, and dBASE
- High level of self-motivation and attention to detail

Job Duties

- Code, test, debug, and maintain programs
- Create program documentation
- Integrate new hardware into existing systems
- Diagnose and correct systems failures
- Maintain monitors, database packages, compilers, assemblers, and utility programs
- Select and modify new hardware and software to company specifications

Achievements

- Designed programs in C Plus for Heritage Bank to coordinate functions of ATM machines
- Purchased new hardware and software for Advantage Publishers, modified equipment to suit company's needs and resolve interoperability issues

Employers

Heritage Bank	June 1999 to Present
Advantage Publishers	March 1996 to June 1999

References

Marta Dalton	Renu Das
Vice President of Finance	Director of Human Resources
Heritage Bank	Advantage Publishers
411 Watkins Street	694 Dale Street
Charleston, WV 25304	Deer Park, NY 11729
(304) 555-2225, Ext. 203	(516) 555-7937

Remember that a resume is not an autobiography. Too much information will only get in the way. The more compact your resume, the easier it will be to review. If a person who is swamped with resumes looks at yours, catches the main points, and then calls you for an interview to fill in some of the details, your resume has already accomplished its task. A clear and concise resume makes for a happy reader and a good impression.

There are times when, despite extensive editing, the resume simply cannot fit on one page. In this case, the resume should be laid out on two pages in such a way that neither clarity nor appearance is compromised. Each page of a two-page resume should be marked clearly: the first should indicate "Page 1 of 2," and the second should include your name and the page number, for example, "Julia Ramirez—Page 2 of 2." The pages should then be stapled together. You may use a smaller font (in the same font as the body of your resume) for the page numbers. Place them at the bottom of page one and the top of page two. Again, spend the time now to experiment with the layout until you find one that looks good to you.

Always show your final layout to other people and ask them what they like or dislike about it, and what impresses them most when they read your resume. Make sure that their responses are the same as what you want to elicit from your prospective employer. If they aren't the same, you should continue to make changes until the necessary information is emphasized.

Proofreading

After you have finished typing the master copy of your resume and before you have it copied or printed, thoroughly check it for typing and spelling errors. Do not place all your trust in your computer's spellcheck function. Use an old editing trick and read the whole resume backward—start at the end and read it right to left and bottom to top. This can help you see the small errors or inconsistencies that are easy to overlook. Take time to do it right because a single error on a document this important can cause the reader to judge your attention to detail in a harsh light.

Have several people look at the finished resume just in case you've missed an error. Don't try to take a shortcut; not having an unbiased set of eyes examine your resume now could mean embarrassment later. Even experienced editors can easily overlook their own errors. Be thorough and conscientious with your proofreading so your first impression is a perfect one.

We have included the following rules of capitalization and punctuation to assist you in the final stage of creating your resume. Remember that resumes often require use of a shorthand style of writing that may include sentences without periods and other stylistic choices that break the standard rules of grammar. Be consistent in each section and throughout the whole resume with your choices.

RULES OF CAPITALIZATION

- Capitalize proper nouns, such as names of schools, colleges, and universities; names of companies; and brand names of products.

- Capitalize major words in the names and titles of books, tests, and articles that appear in the body of your resume.

- Capitalize words in major section headings of your resume.

- Do not capitalize words just because they seem important.

- When in doubt, consult a manual of style such as *Words into Type* (Prentice-Hall) or *The Chicago Manual of Style* (The University of Chicago Press). Your local library can help you locate these and other reference books. Many computer programs also have grammar help sections.

RULES OF PUNCTUATION

- Use commas to separate words in a series.

- Use a semicolon to separate series of words that already include commas within the series. (For an example, see the first rule of capitalization.)

- Use a semicolon to separate independent clauses that are not joined by a conjunction.

- Use a period to end a sentence.

- Use a colon to show that examples or details follow that will expand or amplify the preceding phrase.

- Avoid the use of dashes.

- Avoid the use of brackets.

- If you use any punctuation in an unusual way in your resume, be consistent in its use.

- Whenever you are uncertain, consult a style manual.

Putting Your Resume in Print

You will need to buy high-quality paper for your printer before you print your finished resume. Regular office paper is not good enough for resumes; the reviewer will probably think it looks flimsy and cheap. Go to an office supply store or copy shop and select a high-quality bond paper that will make a good first impression. Select colors like white, off-white, or possibly a light gray. In some industries, a pastel may be acceptable, but be sure the color and feel of the paper makes a subtle, positive statement about you. Nothing in the choice of paper should be loud or unprofessional.

If your computer printer does not reproduce your resume properly and produces smudged or stuttered type, either ask to borrow a friend's or take your disk (or a clean original) to a printer or copy shop for high-quality copying. If you anticipate needing a large number of copies, taking your resume to a copy shop or a printer is probably the best choice.

Hold a sheet of your unprinted bond paper up to the light. If it has a watermark, you will want to point this out to the person helping you with copies; the printing should be done so that the reader can read the print and see the watermark the right way up. Check each copy for smudges or streaks. This is the time to be a perfectionist—the results of your careful preparation will be well worth it.

The Cover Letter

Once your resume has been assembled, laid out, and printed to your satisfaction, the next and final step before distribution is to write your cover letter. Though there may be instances where you deliver your resume in person, you will usually send it through the mail or online. Resumes sent through the mail always need an accompanying letter that briefly introduces you and your resume. The purpose of the cover letter is to get a potential employer to read your resume, just as the purpose of the resume is to get that same potential employer to call you for an interview.

Like your resume, your cover letter should be clean, neat, and direct. A cover letter usually includes the following information:

1. Your name and address (unless it already appears on your personal letterhead) and your phone number(s); see item 7.

2. The date.

3. The name and address of the person and company to whom you are sending your resume.

4. The salutation ("Dear Mr." or "Dear Ms." followed by the person's last name, or "To Whom It May Concern" if you are answering a blind ad).

5. An opening paragraph explaining why you are writing (for example, in response to an ad, as a follow-up to a previous meeting, at the suggestion of someone you both know) and indicating that you are interested in whatever job is being offered.

6. One or more paragraphs that tell why you want to work for the company and what qualifications and experiences you can bring to the position. This is a good place to mention some detail about

that particular company that makes you want to work for them; this shows that you have done some research before applying.

7. A final paragraph that closes the letter and invites the reviewer to contact you for an interview. This can be a good place to tell the potential employer which method would be best to use when contacting you. Be sure to give the correct phone number and a good time to reach you, if that is important. You may mention here that your references are available upon request.

8. The closing ("Sincerely" or "Yours truly") followed by your signature in a dark ink, with your name typed under it.

Your cover letter should include all of this information and be no longer than one page in length. The language used should be polite, businesslike, and to the point. Don't attempt to tell your life story in the cover letter; a long and cluttered letter will serve only to annoy the reader. Remember that you need to mention only a few of your accomplishments and skills in the cover letter. The rest of your information is available in your resume. If your cover letter is a success, your resume will be read and all pertinent information reviewed by your prospective employer.

Producing the Cover Letter

Cover letters should always be individualized because they are always written to specific individuals and companies. Never use a form letter for your cover letter or copy it as you would a resume. Each cover letter should be unique, and as personal and lively as possible. (Of course, once you have written and rewritten your first cover letter until you are satisfied with it, you can certainly use similar wording in subsequent letters. You may want to save a template on your computer for future reference.) Keep a hard copy of each cover letter so you know exactly what you wrote in each one.

There are sample cover letters in Chapter 6. Use them as models or for ideas of how to assemble and lay out your own cover letters. Remember that every letter is unique and depends on the particular circumstances of the individual writing it and the job for which he or she is applying.

After you have written your cover letter, proofread it as thoroughly as you did your resume. Again, spelling or punctuation errors are a sure sign of carelessness, and you don't want that to be a part of your first impression on a prospective employer. This is no time to trust your spellcheck function. Even after going through a spelling and grammar check, your cover letter should be carefully proofread by at least one other person.

Print the cover letter on the same quality bond paper you used for your resume. Remember to sign it, using a good, dark-ink pen. Handle the letter and resume carefully to avoid smudging or wrinkling, and mail them together in an appropriately sized envelope. Many stores sell matching envelopes to coordinate with your choice of bond paper.

Keep an accurate record of all resumes you send out and the results of each mailing. This record can be kept on your computer, in a calendar or notebook, or on file cards. Knowing when a resume is likely to have been received will keep you on track as you make follow-up phone calls.

About a week after mailing resumes and cover letters to potential employers, contact them by telephone. Confirm that your resume arrived and ask whether an interview might be possible. Be sure to record the name of the person you spoke to and any other information you gleaned from the conversation. It is wise to treat the person answering the phone with a great deal of respect; sometimes the assistant or receptionist has the ear of the person doing the hiring.

You should make a great impression with the strong, straightforward resume and personalized cover letter you have just created. We wish you every success in securing the career of your dreams!

Chapter 5

Sample Resumes

This chapter contains dozens of sample resumes for people pursuing a wide variety of communications jobs and careers.

There are many different styles of resumes in terms of graphic layout and presentation of information. These samples also represent people with varying amounts of education and experience. Use these samples to model your own resume after. Choose one resume, or borrow elements from several different resumes to help you construct your own.

SERITA TERESA WOODMAN

4553 N. Alamo Avenue
Dallas, TX 74667
216/555-8908
s.woodman@xxx.com

OBJECTIVE

Public relations representative for a company that markets vacation packages.

EXPERIENCE

American Airlines, Inc., Dallas, TX
Sales Representative, 2000 - present

- Sell reservations for domestic flights, hotels, and car rentals.
- Market travel packages through travel agencies.
- Negotiate airline and hotel discounts for customers.
- Devise itineraries and solve customers' travel-related problems.

Salt Lake Travel, Salt Lake City, UT
Travel Agent, 1996 - 2000

- Handled customer reservations for airlines, hotels, and car rentals.
- Advised customers on competitive travel packages and prices.
- Interacted with all major airlines, hotel chains, and car rental companies.

EDUCATION

University of Illinois, Urbana, IL
B.A. in Anthropology, 1996

SPECIAL SKILLS

- Hands-on experience using most travel-related computer systems including Apollo.
- Working knowledge of German, French, and Polish.

REFERENCES AVAILABLE

Santi Nole

4390 S. Finley
Baton Rouge, LA 20932
Home: 504/555-3892
Santi.Nole@xxx.com

Career Objective   A career in graphic design

Education   University of Louisiana, Baton Rouge, LA
B.A. in Commercial Art, expected June 2003

Experience   Baton Graphics, Baton Rouge, LA
Intern, Summer 2002

University of Louisiana, Baton Rouge, LA
Yearbook Art Director, 2001

Emerge Magazine
Visual Art Editor, 2000

Memberships   Art Directors and Artists Club, 2001 to Present

Awards   First Place, University of Louisiana Student Design
Competition, May 2001

References and portfolio available for review

D A R R Y L   P A N D Y
3300 E. 17th St. #2
St. Louis, MO 54098
314/555-8979

JOB OBJECTIVE
Seeking copywriting position in an advertising agency

SKILLS & ACCOMPLISHMENTS
Writing
- Wrote copy for specific demographics
- Developed ideas and designed ads for magazine, newspaper, and display
- Assisted in the editing of copy for radio jingles
- Produced copy for newsletters and brochures

Research
- Advised on advertising strategies based on competitor information
- Oversaw specific product research and instructed other employees
- Made recommendations and developed plans based on research
- Created consumer profile studies for reference

EMPLOYMENT EXPERIENCE
Porter & Cook, St. Louis, MO
Assistant Copywriter, 2000 - present

EDUCATION
Washington University, St. Louis, MO
B.A. in Advertising, 1999

HONORS
Dean's List, 1998, 1999
Cum Laude, 1999
Jerome T. Coppick Advertising Award, 1998

REFERENCES
Available on request

EUNICE T. BODEANE

1221 E. CAMBRIDGE AVENUE
LYNN, MA 02129
HOME: 617/555-8800
E.BODEANE@XXX.COM

OBJECTIVE: A publicist position with an arts organization.

WORK HISTORY: Boston Opera Company, Boston, MA
                  P.R. Assistant, 2001-Present
                  • Compose press releases and public service
                    announcements to publicize opera events.
                  • Develop contacts with Boston entertainment
                    columnists that result in extensive coverage.
                  • Maintain calendar of advertising deadlines.
                  • Write ad copy for print and radio spots.

                  Sandra Watt Agency, Boston, MA
                  Editorial/P.R. Assistant, 2000-2001
                  • Edited technical and literary manuscripts.
                  • Compiled a directory of Boston editors and
                    publishers for agency use.
                  • Organized an educational workshop for local
                    writers.

EDUCATION: Ithaca University, Ithaca, NY
                  B.S. in Advertising, June 2001

                  Courses included Marketing Techniques, Advertising,
                  Corporate Public Relations, and P.R. Techniques.

HONORS: • Sigma Kappa Nu Honorary Society
                  • Honors in Advertising
                  • Dean's List
                  • Myron T. Kapp Public Relations Award

ACTIVITIES: • Student Government Representative
                  • Homecoming Committee
                  • Soccer Club

REFERENCES: Provided on request.

MICHAEL TURNER

3647 S. Hancock Street • Santa Fe, New Mexico 87501
(505) 555-1776 (Work) • (505) 555-0798 (Home)

GOAL

Opportunity to produce polished technical communications on environmental topics.

EXPERIENCE

- Edited and produced procedure and training manuals for hazardous waste disposal.
- Created an employee training manual for an educational consulting firm specializing in asbestos abatement programs.
- Developed text and maps for the National Parks Service's visitor guides.

EDUCATION

M.A. University of New Mexico   2000
American Studies/Ecology concentration

B.A. University of New Mexico   1998
Technical Communications concentration

WORK HISTORY

1998 to Present   J.S. Spencer Environmental Services
                    Environmental Communications Consultant

1996 to 1998   National Parks Service
                    Student Intern

REFERENCES AVAILABLE

Sam Springfield

666 Plymouth Rd. #444 • Bangor, ME 00099
Home: 207-555-4249 • Sam.Springfield@xxx.com

CAREER OBJECTIVE   A career in graphic design.

EMPLOYMENT   Top Graphics, Bangor, ME
                         Graphic Designer, 2000 - present
                         • Develop and follow accounts from concept through
                           production.
                         • Assemble and log expenses.
                         • Review and approve layout.
                         • Contract and supervise freelance artists.
                         • Operate computerized typesetting equipment.

                         Richmond Register, Richmond, VA
                         Production Manager, 2000 - 2001
                         • Supervised five designers.
                         • Coordinated typesetting and production schedules.
                         • Consistently met deadlines.
                         • Coordinated advertising for daily and Sunday editions.
                         • Maintained supply stock.

                         Staff Designer, 1999 - 2000
                         • Designed and produced editorial and advertising layouts.
                         • Developed and implemented ad strategies.
                         • Created various promotional materials.

                         Springfield Design, Bangor, ME
                         Freelance Designer, 1999 - present
                         • Produce posters, logos, brochures, and ads for a variety of
                           companies and organizations including Bangor High
                           School, United Forestry Inc., the Rotary Club, and the
                           National Kidney Foundation.

EDUCATION   Bangor School of Design, Bangor, ME
                         Studied Advanced Compugraphics, Summer 2001

                         University of Pittsburgh, Pittsburgh, PA
                         Bachelor of Arts in Design, June 1998
                         • Design Honor Award
                         • Photography Honor Award

                         University of Hawaii, Honolulu, HI
                         Studied Liberal Arts, 1995 - 1996

REFERENCES   Available

ROBERTA MORALES

5500 Trenton Road
Shreveport, LA 22909
(318) 555-5900
R.Morales@xxx.com

SKILLS

- Editing
- Writing
- Copyediting
- Content editing
- Proofreading
- Document production
- Understanding of scientific and technical subject matter and industry terms
- Proficient in the current A.P. Style Guide

EXPERIENCE

MARTINDALE PRESS, Shreveport, LA
Assistant Editor, 6/00 to present

- Copyeditor for scientific and technical book publisher.
- Prepare manuscripts for production, conduct photo research, prepare catalog and book cover copy.
- Assist marketing and sales departments on all aspects of book production.
- Represent publisher during trade shows and conventions.

HENDERSON CHEMICAL CORP., New Orleans, LA
Technical Editor, 4/98 to 6/00

- Wrote, edited, and designed reports, work plans, and other technical documents.
- Many documents dealt with safety procedures and hazardous waste management policies.

UNIVERSITY OF NEW ORLEANS, New Orleans, LA
Technical Writer, 1/95 to 3/98

- Created brochures, newsletter articles, feature stories, and press releases on scientific and engineering research being conducted at the university.
- Topics included microbiology, genetic research, and computer modeling.

EDUCATION
University of New Orleans, New Orleans, LA
B.A. in English, December 1994
Minor: Microbiology
Graduated Magna Cum Laude

MEMBERSHIPS
- National Association of Environmental Professionals
- Technical Writers of America
- Earth Team, U.S. Department of Agriculture
- American Association of Editors

REFERENCES
Writing samples and references are available.

LUIS SANCHEZ
4742 N. Lawndale
Chicago, IL 60625
L.Sanchez@xxx.com
773-555-2574

OBJECTIVE
Obtain a position as a video production assistant.

WORK EXPERIENCE
Good's Video, Chicago, IL
Assistant Manager, 2001 - present
- Serve as assistant manager of a full-service video store with supervision of seven sales people.
- Research customers' buying habits and preferences.
- Handle promotion and mailings for special sales and in-store events.
- Help to increase sales by providing personal attention to customer needs.

Johnson Florists, Chicago, IL
Salesperson, 1994 - 2001
- Handled all aspects of sales.
- Greeted customers and advised them on purchases.
- Generated repeat business by building a strong rapport with customers.
- Entered data on computer to keep track of inventory.
- Handled returns and orders from distributor.
- Designed window and floor displays for the showroom.

Mita Co., Chicago, IL
Sales Representative, 1989 - 1994
- Sold and serviced office copiers to businesses and schools in the greater Chicago area.
- Maintained good customer relations through frequent calls and visits.
- Identified and prospected potential customers.

EDUCATION
Northeastern Illinois University, Chicago, IL
- Attended two years.
- Majored in film.

REFERENCE
Available on request.

WENDY ZIMMERMAN

45330 Santa Monica Blvd.
Los Angeles, CA 90088
Home: 213-555-8393
Cellular: 213-555-3839

OBJECTIVE: Editor for a publishing company

EXPERIENCE: Winterpark Publishing Inc., Pasadena, CA
Associate Publisher, 1999 - Present

- Review and evaluate book proposals.
- Acquire new authors and titles.
- Negotiate book contracts.
- Design formats for series and hire writers and editors.
- Assistant with line of travel books currently producing over thirty new titles per year.

Zimmerman Communications, Inc., Los Angeles, CA
Freelance Writer, 1997 - 1999

- Produced a variety of projects for freelance clients.
- Edited technical manuals explaining computer software.
- Scripted four industrial films for various food service companies.
- Composed copy for department store catalog.
- Created newsletters and brochures.

EDUCATION: UCLA, Los Angeles, CA
B.A. in English, 1997

HONORS: Phi Beta Kappa, 1997
Second Prize, Robert D. Mayo Writing Contest

REFERENCES: On Request

Michelle Cook

640 S. Long Street   Home (617) 555-5306
Boston, MA 02116   Work (617) 555-1202
                                                    M.L.Cook@xxx.com

Expertise

Editorial
Experienced content and copy editor with specialization in scientific topics. Trained and experienced in desktop publisher, QuarkXPress and PageMaker. Accurate proofreader and familiar with the A.P. Style Guide.

Teaching
Certified secondary teacher with experience teaching biology and chemistry.

Research
Competent research assistant with strong lab skills and experience in statistical analysis.

Employers

Journal of American Science
Assistant Editor, 1999 to Present

St. Steven's Academy
Science Teacher, 1998 to 1999

University of Maryland
Department of Biology
Laboratory Assistant, 1997

Education

B.S., University of Maryland, June 1998
Majored in Education with a Biology minor

REGINA REGAN JOHNSON

70652 Fern Dell Drive • Glenview, IL 60067 • 708-555-4928
R.Johnson@xxx.com

WRITING EXPERIENCE

Screenplays

Completed spec screenplay, *Carnival*, and treatments for forthcoming spec screenplays: *Harold and Fred*, *Dream House*, *The Outsider*, *Job-Hunting*, *The Adventures of Little Leon*, and *The Carpet Sweeper*.

Children's Books

Wrote *Hats* (now in revision at Houghton Mifflin, Boston, MA) and *The Carpet Sweeper*.

Short Stories

Wrote *A Garden* - collected short stories and two one-act plays.

Published

Published twice in *The Christian Science Monitor* on the "Home Forum" and "Home and Family" pages. Published poems and children's articles in *The Christian Science Sentinel*.

PROFESSIONAL MEMBERSHIPS

Participating as a full member in:
- Women in Film
- Society of Children's Book Writers
- Associate member: Society of Midland Authors

EDUCATION

Northwestern University, Evanston, IL
Received B.A. in English, June 2002.
- Majored in Theatre and English for three years at Northwestern University, then returned to Northwestern after rearing two sons to complete B.A. degree in English.
- Admitted to the writing program and studied fiction writing with Jonathon Brent and playwriting with David Rush.
- Recently completed a graduate course in feature film writing with Mary-Therese Cozzola at Northwestern University.

References are available.

Rosemary Deborah Parker
5509 E. George Street, Apt. 442
Columbia, SC 29263
803-555-2893

Career Objective
Obtain a position as a magazine editor

Skills & Accomplishments
- Evaluated submitted manuscripts for a monthly magazine.
- Handled copyediting and rewriting of manuscripts.
- Worked with artists and designers on layout aspects.
- Supervised the publication of an anthology of poetry.
- Served as proofreader for feature articles.
- Handled copyediting duties for local newspaper.
- Reported on events of local interest.
- Represented employer at several publishing conferences.

Employment History
Carolina Woman, Columbia, SC
Assistant Editor, 2000 - present

Raleigh *Gazette*, Raleigh, NC
Copyeditor/Reporter, 1999 - 2000

Education
Columbia University, Columbia, SC
B.A. in Journalism, June 1999
Minor in English

Honors
- Summa Cum Laude
- Journalism Award, 1999
- Henry Moffatt Scholarship Recipient, 1997 - 1999

References available upon request

JONNI KARBERST

144 Woodbine, Apt. 45 • Albuquerque, NM 88299
505-555-4909 • karberst@xxx.com

CAREER OBJECTIVE
Obtain a position in the graphic design field

EMPLOYMENT HISTORY
Graphic Designer, 2000 - present
Fox Graphics, Albuquerque, NM
- Manage accounts from concept through production
- Track expenses and budget
- Oversee and approve layout
- Contract freelance artists

Production Manager, 1999 - 2000
Arizona Register, **Phoenix, AZ**
- Supervised staff of five designers
- Coordinated typesetting and camera schedules
- Consistently met tight deadlines
- Coordinated advertising for daily and Sunday editions
- Maintained supply stock

Staff Designer, 1998 - 1999
Arizona Register, **Phoenix, AZ**
- Designed and produced editorial and advertising layouts
- Developed and implemented ad strategies
- Created promotional materials

Freelance Designer, 1998 - present
Mink Design, Phoenix, AZ, and Albuquerque, NM
- Produce posters, logos, brochures, and ads for a variety of organizations

EDUCATION
Albuquerque School of Design, Albuquerque, NM
Studied Advanced Compugraphics, Summer 2001

University of Arizona, Phoenix, AZ
Bachelor of Arts in Design, 1998
- Design Honor Award
- Photography Honor Award

University of Nevada, Carson City, NV
Studied liberal arts, 1994 - 1996

References Available

THOMAS BERGMAN

988 Wilmington Road • Chattanooga, TN 75221 • 615-555-4948
T.Bergman@xxx.com

OVERVIEW   *Recent graduate of University of Tennessee's journalism program.
Extensive internship experience in all areas of communications.
Seeking opportunity to use writing, editing, and research skills in
the communications industry.*

SKILLS   *Media*
Experience in television production
Extensive research skills
Television news knowledge

Journalism
Editorial and production experience
Excellent writing, editing, and layout skills
Reporting experience
Magazine and newspaper experience

Advertising
Broad copywriting background
Demographic research experience
Editing, proofreading, and ad production skills

EMPLOYERS   News Division, WCN-TV, Chattanooga, TN
Research Assistant, Summer 2001

Southern Style Magazine, Atlanta, GA
Student Intern, Summer 2000

Chattanooga Gazette
Intern, Summer 1999

Prentiss Advertising
Junior Copywriter, Summer 1998

EDUCATION   University of Tennessee at Chattanooga
B.A. in Journalism, May 2002

HONORS   Knoxville Journalism Scholarship
Dean's List

REFERENCES   Writing samples and references are available.

LISA SMITH

428 Elm Street • Des Plaines, IL 60016 • Lisa.Smith@xxx.com • 847-555-4098

CAREER GOAL

Obtain a position as an advertising copywriter

EDUCATION

B.A. in English
Knox College, Galesburg, IL
June 2000

EXPERIENCE

Copywriter, June 2000 to Present
H & J Book Publishers, Chicago, IL

- Create copy for ad campaigns designed to promote textbook publisher's line of books in trade magazine and newspapers.
- Assist marketing and editorial departments with sell copy for book catalogs, direct mail pieces, and trade show materials.
- Excellent attention to detail and respect for deadlines; creative approaches to projects within dictated structure set by advertising management.

Student Intern, Summer 1996
Mellon Advertising, Skokie, IL

- Assisted advertising executives in creating point-of-purchase displays.
- Participated in design development sessions with clients.
- Worked with graphic artists to create caption copy.

REFERENCES

Available

MICHAEL ERVIN MCDONALD

333 E. RHETT DRIVE • AUGUSTA, GA 33390
404-555-0393 • M.E.MCDONALD@XXX.COM

OBJECTIVE

Program director of a major market urban radio station.

EXPERIENCE

WGAU Radio, Augusta, GA
Producer/Announcer, 1998-present
- Produced weekly jazz music show for a noncommercial radio station.
- Determined play list and weekly ads for show.
- Placed special emphasis on African-American artists and their work.
- Developed special feature segments.
- Served as show's host.

WROB Radio, Robinson, IL
Program Director/Music Director, 1996-1998
- Coordinated and presented the complete daily program schedule for a non-commercial radio station which emphasized jazz music and public affairs.
- Arranged work schedule for the entire staff.
- Conducted planning meetings.
- Made production assignments.
- Selected music to fit station's format with the goal of increasing listenership.

WREE Radio, East St. Louis, IL
Producer/Announcer, 1990-1995
- Produced two weekend jazz shows for a noncommercial radio station.
- Served as announcer for both shows.
- Interviewed contemporary jazz artists.
- Researched and selected music for other jazz shows at the station.

Top Street Records, East St. Louis, IL
Sales Clerk, 1985-1990
- Handled inventory and sales for jazz department.
- Ordered records based on weekly sales reports.
- Conducted music research for two local radio stations.
- Instituted marketing plan for department, which resulted in a 25% increase in sales quarterly.

EDUCATION

Midwest School of Broadcasting, St. Louis, MO
Certificate, 1985

East St. Louis High School, East St. Louis, IL
Graduated, 1984

Peter Klept

554 Grambling Road
Santa Barbara, CA 97770

Peter.Klept@xxx.com
814-555-5009

Goal

Full-time employment as an audio control technician

Qualifications

Certificate of Completion, June 2001
Communications Technology Institute, Santa Barbara

- Specialization: Broadcast Technology
- Radiotelephone Operator Permit #555-5555
- Member of the National Association of Broadcasters

Work History

Audio Control Technician
August 2002 to Present
WKET, Santa Barbara

Recording Technician
July 2001 to August 2002
WKET, Santa Barbara

Skills

- Proficient in ProTools
- Familiar with analog tape editing procedure
- Comfortable in a professional recording setting

References

Available on request

GLORIA GARLAND

1220 MARKET STREET #3 • SAN FRANCISCO, CA 92290

(415) 555-5508 • GARLAND@XXX.COM

OBJECTIVE

A management-level position in the publishing industry.

WORK EXPERIENCE

Bay Magazine, **San Francisco, CA**
Regional Manager, 1999 - present
- Oversee administration, negotiation, and maintenance of exchange agreements and sales promotion.
- Track market changes with responsibility for executing responses to developments.
- Recently led magazine's eastern edition through a reorganization period.
- Planned and implemented new editions in the south.

Sandler Imports, Sausalito, CA
Sales Coordinator, 1995 - 1999
- Managed ten field representatives.
- Handled information dissemination and distribution.
- Co-designed a full-color catalog.
- Placed advertising in major trade publications.
- Promoted products at trade shows.
- Maintained inventory status reports and personnel records.

Redwood Publishing Co., San Francisco, CA
Distribution Assistant, 1990 - 1995
- Developed new distribution outlets through cold calls and follow-up visits.
- Increased distribution in my district by 45% over a three-year period.
- Coordinated a direct mail program that increased magazine subscriptions by 120%.

Xerox Co., Atlanta, CA
Sales Representative, 1987 - 1990
- Sold and serviced office copiers to businesses and schools in the greater Atlanta area.
- Maintained good customer relations through frequent calls and visits.
- Identified potential customers.

EDUCATION

Miami University, Miami, OH
B.S. in Communications, 1987

PROFESSIONAL MEMBERSHIPS

- National Association of Importers
- Sausalito Community Association
- San Francisco Chamber of Commerce
- American Publishing Association

SEMINARS

- "Publishing in the '90s," Chicago, IL
- "International Publishing," New York, NY

REFERENCES

Available on request.

James Thornborough Newton

1171 Davis St., #2
Evanston, IL 60202
E-mail: JTNewton@xxx.com
Cellular: 847-555-6684

Objective

Staff writer/researcher for the news department of a newspaper where I can utilize my editorial, writing, and reporting skills.

Education

Northwestern University, Evanston, IL
   B.A. in Journalism & Political Science (double major)
   Summa Cum Laude, June 2000

Accomplishments

- Wrote a weekly column on political issues for campus newspaper.
- Won two journalism awards for a feature series titled "The Nuclear Threat."
- Interviewed newsworthy people in the community.
- Covered local news events.
- Researched and wrote pamphlets for the Evanston City Council on crime, pollution, gentrification, and zoning.
- Edited grant proposals for the local theater company.
- Served as an assistant researcher for NBC opinion poll.

Employment History

The Daily Northwestern, Evanston, IL
Staff Writer, 1998-2000

Evanston City Council, Evanston, IL
Researcher/Writer, 1999-2000

Victory Gardens Theater, Chicago, IL
Editor, 1998

NBC-TV, Chicago, IL
Researcher, 1998

References and Writing Samples

Available on request

TINA HERNANDEZ
329 Kedzie Avenue, Apt. #2 ◆ Evanston, IL 60202 ◆ Home: 847-555-4727

WRITING EXPERIENCE
Arco Publishing Group, Chicago, IL
Book Writer, 1999 - present
- Author of *Environmental Impact* and *Home Improvements.*

National College of Education, Evanston, IL
Editor, Grants Department, 1999
- Edited grant proposals and created brochures on grant programs.

Stagebill Magazine, New York, NY
Feature Writer, 1998 - 1999

Rapport Theater, Chicago, IL
Editor/Research Assistant, 1997 - 1998
- Researched, compiled, and edited study guides for seven productions.

OTHER WORK EXPERIENCE
Northwestern University, Evanston, IL
Administrative Assistant, 1997 - 1999
- Drafted and edited correspondence.
- Managed expense accounts and monitored monthly budgets.
- Handled scheduling of appointments and preparation of course materials.

Rapport Theater, Chicago, IL
Office Manager, 1995 - 1997
- Maintained payroll and financial records.
- Interviewed, selected, and supervised work-study students.
- Organized and monitored registration for Theater Center classes.

EDUCATION
Northwestern University, Evanston, IL
- Bachelor of Arts with Honors in English, June 1995
- Cumulative G.P.A.: 3.76

HONORS
- Phi Beta Kappa
- Honors in English
- Dean's List, seven quarters
- Mayo Writing Prize, Honorable Mention, 1993

REFERENCES AND WRITING SAMPLES AVAILABLE

HARRISON CRUMB

3338 W. Redbook Drive   Home: (806) 555-1910
Amarillo, TX 78077   Pager: (806) 555-7730

JOB SOUGHT
Director of Traffic at the WXBZ television station.

WORK EXPERIENCE
WRMC-TV, Amarillo, TX
Assistant Director of Traffic, 1998 - present
- Act as a liaison between syndication companies and station.
- Create the daily TV log.
- Establish sales availabilities.
- Screen and process tapes and films.
- Pull and disseminate teletype information.

WPIX-TV, El Paso, TX
Assistant to the Traffic Director, 1996 - 1998
- Handled maintenance of traffic boards.
- Filed and updated TV logs.
- Prepared advance program information for TV listings.
- Ordered films and tapes for future use.
- Organized processing procedure for PSAs.

Assistant to Head Programmer, 1995 - 1996
- Oversaw program scheduling.
- Updated and maintained TV log.
- Handled public service spots.
- Routed correspondence for Head Programmer.

EDUCATION
B.A. in Communications, Amarillo State College, May 1995
- Focus on Television

MEMBERSHIPS
- Texas Communications Association
- Amarillo Citizens Council

References available

MARY ALICE MOORE

3230 W. ALSIP DRIVE #3C • MILWAUKEE, WI 53100
HOME: 419/555-8908 • E-MAIL: M.MOORE@XXX.COM

OBJECTIVE: *Public relations assistant for major U.S. airline*

EXPERIENCE: **Midwest Airlines, Inc., Milwaukee, WI**
Sales Representative, 1999 - present
- Reservation sales for domestic flights, hotels, and car rentals.
- Market travel packages through travel agencies.
- Negotiate hotel and airline discounts for customers.
- Create itineraries and solve customers' travel-related problems.

Travel in the Main, Evanston, IL
Travel Agent, 1991 - 1999
- Handled customer reservations for airlines, hotels, and car rentals.
- Advised customers on competitive travel packages and prices.
- Interacted with all major airlines, hotel chains, and car rental companies.

EDUCATION: **Oakton Community College, Des Plaines, IL**
Travel Industry Training Program
Certificate of Completion, June 1991

University of Wisconsin, Beloit, WI
B.A. in Anthropology, 1987

SKILLS: Hands-on experience using most travel-related computer systems, including Apollo.

Working knowledge of German, French, and Polish.

REFERENCES: Available on request.

GERALD SCHWARTZ

10 Downing St. #230 • Detroit, MI 53309
Home: 313/555-0009 • E-mail: G.Schwartz@xxx.com

JOB OBJECTIVE

Obtain an entry-level position in a multimedia production company

ACCOMPLISHMENTS

GRAPHIC DESIGN
* Created concept and layouts
* Completed mechanicals for brochures, posters, and books
* Managed production department of publishing company
* Oversaw typography, printing, and binding

AUDIOVISUAL
* Shot still photographs for a pictorial essay
* Served as freelance photographer for various publications
* Handled portrait work and advertising photography
* Completed training in computer graphics and multi-image graphics

WRITING
* Edited course catalogs for a university
* Contributed articles to campus newspaper
* Reviewed manuscripts for publisher

WORK HISTORY

Helicon Publishing, Inc., Detroit, MI
Production Manager, 1998 - present

Freelance Graphic Designer and Photographer, Detroit, MI
1997 - present

Delbert Advertising, Inc., Saginaw, MI
Graphic Designer, 1995 - 1997

Page 1 of 2

EDUCATION

Detroit School of Design, Detroit, MI
Compugraphics, Photography, May 1992

Saginaw College, Saginaw, MI
B.A. in Art, June 1990

FREELANCE CLIENTS

- New Age Books, Madison, WI
- Trends in Design, New York, NY
- Detroit Free Press, Detroit, MI

HONORS

Leadership Award
Midwest Publishers Conference, Spring 1997

Best of Show Award
Detroit School of Design Annual Photo Exhibit, 1992

REFERENCES AVAILABLE UPON REQUEST

William Harris
P.O. Box 4112
Fargo, ND 52289
701/555-3930
Bill.Harris@xxx.com

Radio Experience

WND-RADIO, Fargo, ND
ASSISTANT GENERAL MANAGER, 2000 - 2001

- Assisted in the management of a student-run college radio station.
- Helped to direct and supervised the Board of Directors and an on-air staff to ensure efficient day-to-day operations.
- Established music format guidelines and made other management decisions.
- Wrote and edited budget proposals.

WND-RADIO, Fargo, ND
ALTERNATIVE MUSIC DIRECTOR, 1998 - 2000

- Created and implemented station alternative music format.
- Managed, scheduled, and trained a staff with the station.
- Served as on-air personality.

Education

FARGO COLLEGE, Fargo, ND
B.S. in Business Administration, 2001
Minor in Music

References

Provided on request.

Freelance Writing, Editing & Research

GERMANIA REDSON

666 Torn Leaf Rd. • Hagerstown, MD 03394 • 301-555-3921

FREELANCE EXPERIENCE

WRITING/EDITING
- Served as editor for a series of books on cooking.
- Collaborated on writing and editing projects for a public relations firm.
- Edited a book on international travel published in both English and Spanish.
- Published articles in magazines and newspapers.

RESEARCH
- Researched and compiled bibliographies for several books.
- Interviewed musicians and songwriters for background for book on the music industry.
- Managed references services at a university library.
- Conducted extensive research on the health insurance industry for brochures.

BOOK EVALUATION
- Evaluated manuscripts and produced reader's reports for three publishers.
- Reviewed selected books for local publications.
- Wrote a monthly book review column for community newsletter.

EMPLOYMENT HISTORY

1998 to Present	*Freelance Writer/Editor* - Hagerstown, MD
1994 to 1998	*Librarian*, University of Maryland - Princess Ann, MD
1986 to 1994	*Assistant*, Hagerstown Public Library - Hagerstown, MD
1984 to 1986	*Salesperson*, Poppy Books - Watersford, CT

EDUCATION

University of Maryland - Princess Ann, MD
- B.A. in History with a minor in English, 1984
- M.A. in Library Science, 1986

AFFILIATIONS

- New England Women in Publishing
- American Writers' Association

LISA STANSFIELD

14 E. Three Penny Road   Home: (313) 555-3489
Detroit, MI 33290   L.Stansfield@xxx.com

OBJECTIVE

*A management position in public relations where I can utilize
my promotion and marketing experience.*

WORK EXPERIENCE

SEVEN ELEVEN, INC., Detroit, MI
Marketing Director, 2000 - present
- Developed a successful marketing campaign for a convenience store chain.
- Initiated and maintained a positive working relationship with radio and print media.
- Implemented marketing strategies to increase sales at less profitable outlets.
- Designed a training program for store managers and staff.

SUPER VACUUM CO., Bloomfield Hills, MI
Marketing Representative, 1996 - 2000
- Demonstrated vacuums in specialty and department stores.
- Reported customer reactions to manufacturers.
- Designed fliers and advertising to promote products.
- Oversaw other retail outlets.

REBO CARPETS, INC., Chicago, IL
Assistant Sales Manager, 1991 -1996
- Handled both internal and external areas of sales and marketing including samples, advertising, and pricing.
- Served as company sales representative and sold carpeting to retail outlets.

EDUCATION

University of Michigan, Ann Arbor, MI
B.A. Marketing, 1992

SEMINARS

Michigan Marketing Workshop, 2000 and 2001
Sales and Marketing Association Seminars, 1998

References available on request.

Randall C. Caldwell
6500 Rivercomb Drive #422
Washington, DC 01990
202/555-4421

Objective
A career in the advertising industry.

Education
Georgetown University
B.A. in Advertising
June 2002

Studied: Advertising, Marketing, Graphic Arts, Journalism,
    and Business

Skills & Accomplishments
- Handled four accounts for advertising agency.
- Assisted with traffic control.
- Served as intermediary between client and account executives.
- Assisted in writing copy and designing ads for magazine copy.
- Computed ad sizes.
- Answered clients' questions.
- Wrote feature articles on community news including education, sports, politics, and the arts.
- Provided photos and illustration for articles.

Work Experience
Simon & Simon, Inc., Baltimore, MD
Advertising Intern, 2001

Capitol Life Magazine, Washington, DC
Advertising Assistant, Part-Time, 2000

Washington News, New Brunswick, ME
Freelance Writer, 1999 - 2001

Honors
Summa Cum Laude, 2002
Dean's List
Winterburg Scholarship, 2001

References Provided on Request

Jacob Rosenthal   **Community Relations/Media Specialist**

2950 W. Best Road
Raleigh, North Carolina 27695
J.Rosenthal@xxx.com
(303) 442-5284

Overview

Self-employed communications professional with extensive experience assisting both private and nonprofit agencies promote their services and maintain a positive image in the community.

Work History

Owner, Rosenthal Communications, 1998 to present
- Manage successful freelance business with clients including the City of Raleigh, Raleigh General Hospital, North Carolina State University, Carleton Community College, and Riverside Amusement Corporation.
- Design complete publicity packages to inform community of available services, promote corporate identity, and increase sales.
- Write press releases, brochures, ad copy, feature articles, and statements to press.
- Produce radio and cable TV spots.
- Develop concepts and goals with clients and manage all details while supervising subcontractors as necessary and keeping client abreast of progress.

Community Services Director, 1996 to 1998, North Carolina State University
- Directed numerous community outreach programs.
- Conducted needs assessments and worked in conjunction with academic faculty and administrative staff to meet the needs of diverse learners.
- Created distance learning options and promoted new programs through local and national media.
- Arranged off-site course locations for evening division courses.

Production Assistant, 1994 to 1996, WNC-TV
- Assisted in production of wide variety of community access programming, including children's and educational television.
- Assisted producers on-site with setups and breakdowns of shoots.
- Edited footage.
- Produced promotional spots and public service announcements.

Education

B.A. in Communications, North Carolina State University, 1994

References

References and portfolio of work are available for review.

GERALD ROBERT SCAMPI

4890 W. 57th Street

New York, NY 10019

G.R.Scampi@xxx.com

(212) 555-3678

OBJECTIVE
Vice President of promotion for communications company.

EXPERIENCE
1997-Present   Promotion Manager, ATLANTIC RECORDS, New York, NY

❖ Develop and execute all marketing strategy for record promotion in New York, New Jersey, and Massachusetts.
❖ Interface with sales department and retail stores to ensure adequate product placement.
❖ Attend various company-sponsored sales, marketing, and management seminars.

1990-1997   Promotion Manager, RSO RECORDS, Miami, FL

❖ Planned all marketing strategy for record promotions in the southeast U.S.
❖ Worked closely with sales and touring bands to ensure product visibility in the marketplace.

1988-1990   On-Air Personality and Music Director, WCFL RADIO, Chicago, IL

❖ Played CHR music.
❖ Made TV and public events appearances for the station.
❖ Organized and staffed station's news department.
❖ Promoted to Music Director after one year.

1985-1988   Program Director, Music Director, and News Director, WGLT RADIO, Atlanta, GA

EDUCATION
1983-1985   Columbia College, Chicago, IL
                     Studied Audio Engineering

REFERENCES AVAILABLE

Sandra Sweeney

1401 N. La Brea Avenue
Hollywood, CA 90028
Home: 213-555-1298
Sandy.Sweeney@xxx.com

Goal

To obtain a position as a traffic manager for an advertising agency in the corporate advertising department.

Work History

1999-Present   *Music Connection Magazine,* **Burbank, CA**
Assistant Production Manager

- Supervise all aspects of production and printing for national publication.
- Involved in heavy client and agency contact.
- Organize all art, layouts, and production details.
- Produce ad copy.

1995-1999   **Circuit City, Hollywood, CA**
Assistant to Promotion Director

- Conducted all in-store promotions and events.
- Placed advertising and publicity in local publications.
- Consulted on grand opening of Santa Monica store.
- Assisted customers frequently.

Education

University of Southern California, Los Angeles, CA
B.S. in Marketing, June 1995

Whitley School of Design, Hollywood, CA
Magazine Production and Design
Certificate of Completion, May 1999

References Available

PERRY WATKINS

5020 Castro Street • San Francisco, CA 99888
E-mail: P.Watkins@xxx.com • Home: (415) 555-3800

WORK EXPERIENCE

HOUSEWISE MAGAZINE, San Francisco, CA
Director of Operations, 1995 to Present
- Supervise 30 regional managers and offices with 519 employees.
- Direct all local operations including circulation, advertising, sales, promotion/marketing, and $22 million salary and budget administration.
- Increased ad sales by $7 million, an 18 percent increase over three years.

Assistant to Editorial Manager, 1988 to 1995
- Coordinated all of magazine's configuration changes.
- Served as operations liaison to Housewise International.
- Initiated subscription sales programs and formulated marketing strategies.
- Developed and implemented all edition modifications in order to boost circulation and optimize advertising sales.

KEYBOARD MAGAZINE, Los Angeles, CA
Assistant Publisher, 1982 to 1988
- Reduced magazine to standard size, which resulted in a substantial reduction in paper and production costs.
- Helped magazine to meet the changing needs of readership and advertisers.
- Supervised an office of eleven.

Advertising Manager, 1975 to 1982
- Generated $300,000 in advertising revenues.
- Increased consumer awareness of the magazine, which led to increased sales.
- Stabilized downward trends in circulation.

EDUCATION

M.A. in Journalism, University of Iowa, 1975
B.A. in History, Barton University, 1973

PROFESSIONAL MEMBERSHIPS

- Entertainment Publishers Society
- National Association of Magazine Publishers
- Castro Neighborhood Improvement Committee

REFERENCES AVAILABLE ON REQUEST

Jeannette Hobbs

843 Magnolia Court, Apt. 2 • Dallas, TX 73389
Cellular: 206-555-1890 • J.Hobbs@xxx.com

Objective   *To obtain a position as an assistant director of public relations*

Employment   **Six Flags Over Texas, Dallas, TX**
Assistant to Director of Public Relations,
2000 - present
- Prepare news releases
- Maintain personal media contacts
- Prepare and edit copy for brochures, ads, and posters
- Help to develop advertising plans.
- Write and edit copy for newsletters
- Prepare and distribute newsletters to patrons
- Handle all booking for live entertainment

Six Flags Over Texas, Dallas, TX
Office Manger, 1997 - 2000
- Coordinated workshops and seminars on publicity
- Handled group travel and hotel arrangements
- Supervised an office staff of eight
- Organized staff meetings
- Booked convention space and planned special events
- Prepared financial reports and handled budgets

Education   Brooklyn College, Brooklyn, NY
B.A. in English Literature, 1996

Skills   - Proficient in the Microsoft Office Suite including Word, Access, PowerPoint, and Excel
- Familiar with numerous customized computer programs
- Adept at using a variety of online research resources
- Knowledge of A.P. Style Guide

References   Available on request

BRIAN WONG

546 Elm Street
Chicago, IL 60645
312-555-3894
B.Wong@xxx.com

GOAL

Computer science professional with experience in customer service and technical writing seeks customer service position with potential for supervisory responsibility.

WORK HISTORY

Technical Writer, February 1997 to Present
Advantage Software Products, Chicago, IL
- ✔ Prepare technical manuals for end users of Advantage Software Products.
- ✔ Obtain program feature specifications from programmers and systems engineers to develop step-by-step instructions, written in clear, nontechnical language.
- ✔ Supervise ongoing revision and updating of manuals.
- ✔ Product line includes desktop publishing, graphic arts, word processing, and database products.

Customer Service Technician, April 1993 to February 1997
Westmont Software, Palatine, IL
- ✔ Provided customer support contact for end users of Westmont Software.
- ✔ Telephone troubleshooter for clients, providing step-by-step solutions for online difficulties.
- ✔ Maintained phone log of customer problems.
- ✔ Worked with systems engineers and technical writers to modify systems designs and revise instructional manuals as necessary.

EDUCATION

University of Illinois at Chicago - One-year Computer Career Training Program
Graduate Certificate, completed January 1997

Northern Illinois University
B.S. Degree, completed January 1996

REFERENCES AVAILABLE

GEORGE T. BENSON

1800 W. Pico • Santa Monica, CA 90110
Home: 213/555-8938 • Cellular: 213/555-8000

JOB OBJECTIVE

A public relations position in the entertainment industry where I can utilize my communications skills, contacts, and industry background.

WORK EXPERIENCE

Independent Marketing, TBC Marketing, Burbank, CA, 1996 - present
➤ Coordinate stock with regional distributors.
➤ Generate exposure and interest at local retail store and one-stops in conjunction with local and regional airplay.
➤ Suggest supplemental marketing strategies based on airplay, sales, and percentage of penetration.

Coordinator of National Marketing, *Hits Magazine*, Van Nuys, CA, 1995 - 1996
➤ Sold charts and tracking information to radio, artist management, and record labels.
➤ Handled tracking for all accounts on charting product.
➤ Interacted with radio accounts weekly regarding early chart information.

Regional Sales Representative, *Cashbox Magazine*, Los Angeles, CA, 1992 - 1995
➤ Developed and managed the West Coast territory for Cashbox Service Network.
➤ Provided chart information, including bullet criteria, points, and sales/airplay ratios, to independent marketing companies and management.
➤ Serviced retail accounts and created new marketing strategies for product tracking services.

Sales Representative, Parker Manufacturing, Flint, MI, 1988 - 1992
➤ Negotiated and sold contract repairs on industrial equipment.
➤ Wrote daily technical reports on product movement and inventory.
➤ Met and exceeded sales quotas for each quarter.

EDUCATION

Michigan State University, East Lansing, MI
B.A., Communications, 1988

SAM GARRISON

83 Main Place #3B • Portland, ME 04129 • 207/555-2321

OBJECTIVE

A position as an advertising assistant where I can use my advertising, marketing, and graphic arts skills.

EDUCATION

University of Maine, New Brunswick, ME
B.A. in Advertising, expected June 2003
Major Fields: Advertising, Marketing, Graphic Arts, Journalism, Business

HONORS

Dean's List
Worthington Academic Merit Scholarship

WORK EXPERIENCE

Lee J. Harris, Inc., Bangor, ME
Advertising Intern, Summer 2002
- Handled four accounts for advertising agency.
- Designed and laid out ads.
- Researched and wrote copy.
- Assisted with all aspects of traffic control.
- Served as liaison between client and account executives.

***Bangor Life Magazine*, Bangor, ME**
Advertising Assistant, part-time, 2001
- Assisted in designing ads for magazine copy.
- Gained experience with Adobe Illustrator and Adobe Photoshop programs.
- Provided basic pricing and design information to clients.

***New Brunswick Daily*, New Brunswick, ME**
Freelance Writer, 1999 to 2001
- Wrote feature articles on local community news, including education, sports, politics, and the arts.
- Provided photos and illustrations in support of various articles.

REFERENCES

References and portfolio are available.

Ned Ramos

197 Compton Street
Chicago, IL 60618
(312) 555-6978
N.Ramos@xxx.com

Work History

Director of Education and Community Relations, **10/00 to Present**
Midwest Science Center
- Develop and implement all staff training and in-service programming.
- Supervise publication of in-house newsletter, press releases, and educational literature.
- Design and direct marketing/community relations campaigns and special events.
- Media contact/museum spokesperson.

Marketing Manager, **8/94 to 10/00**
Baker & West Healthcare Systems
- Directed marketing efforts for multinational medical equipment firm.
- Managed staff of 14 marketing professionals.
- Developed marketing surveys and compiled statistics.
- Issued press releases.
- Designed multimedia campaigns in support of new product.

Technical Writer, **6/90 to 8/94**
Baker & West Healthcare Systems
- Developed equipment product literature including pharmaceutical inserts, technical manuals, and brochures.
- Edited marketing literature.

Education

Bachelor of Arts, Technical Communications, 1990
University of Delaware

Credentials

- Member, Society of Technical Writers
- Member, American Marketing Association

References available

RITA WESTERBURG

3201 W. Oerono Street, Apt. 23 • Pittsburgh, PA 28901 • Office: 412-555-9302

JOB SOUGHT: Public relations director for the marketing division of a major candy manufacturer.

EXPERIENCE:

Public Relations
- Represented company to clients and retailers in order to present new products.
- Organized and planned convention displays and strategy.
- Designed and executed direct mail campaigns that identified marketplace needs and new options for products.

Management
- Managed an entire sales/marketing staff, which included account managers and sales representatives.
- Monitored and studied the effectiveness of a national distribution network.
- Oversaw all aspects of the sales and marketing budget.

Development
- Conceived ads, posters, and point-of-purchase materials for products.
- Initiated and published a monthly newsletter that was distributed to current and potential customers.

EMPLOYMENT: **Redboy Peanut Crunch, Pittsburgh, PA**
National Sales Manager, 1995 - present
Account Manager, 1993 - 1995
Assistant Account Manager 1992 - 1993
Personal Assistant, 1990 - 1992
Receptionist, 1988 - 1990

EDUCATION: B.A. in English, May 1988
University of Pennsylvania, Harrisburg, PA

SKILLS: Proficient in Microsoft Office 2000
Skilled in numerous customized software packages
Versed in current marketing and P.R. strategies

JOEL JAMES

1441 S. Goebert
Providence, RI 00231
Home: 401/555-1234
Cellular: 401/555-3782

OBJECTIVE

To obtain a position as the president of a U.S. publishing corporation where I can apply my extensive management, promotion, and sales experience.

EMPLOYMENT HISTORY

JOHNSON PUBLISHING CORPORATION, Providence, RI
VICE-PRESIDENT, 1995 - Present
- ▼ Promoted from Sales Manager to Vice-President of Advertising after three years.
- ▼ Managed all phases of publishing properties including:
  Furniture Magazine
  Home Improvement Weekly
  Scuba Digest
  Travel Age Magazine
  Pharmacy News
- ▼ Established and developed the first newspaper advertising mat service in the furniture industry. Increased distributors and retailers using this service by 55% in three years.
- ▼ Improved the effectiveness and volume of all retail advertising.

REBUS PUBLISHING COMPANY, Boston, MA
ADVERTISING MANAGER, 1986 - 1994
- ▼ Serviced and developed accounts throughout the eastern United States.
- ▼ Handled advertising for publications in the restaurant industry.
- ▼ Increased sales in my territories every year by at least 21%.

TIME MAGAZINE, New York, NY
ASSISTANT ADVERTISING PROMOTIONS MANAGER, 1984 - 1986
- ▼ Spearheaded original promotion program that increased revenue by 33% in two years.
- ▼ Developed new markets.
- ▼ Helped to improve company/customer relations.

ROYAL CROWN COLA CORPORATION, Chicago, IL
DIVISION SALES MANAGER, 1981 - 1984
 ▼ Promoted from salesperson to sales manager after one year.
 ▼ Organized sampling campaigns and in-store and restaurant displays.
 ▼ Directed bottlers' cooperative advertising and point-of-purchase displays.

EDUCATION

B.A. in Economics, 1980
Drake University, Des Moines, IA
 ▼ Graduated Phi Beta Kappa
 ▼ Top 5% of class

PROFESSIONAL AFFILIATIONS

Rocking Chair, social and professional organization of the furniture industry
President, 1995 - Present

Beverage Association of America
Board of Directors

Publishers Association
Advisory Committee

REFERENCES

Available upon request

GEORGE GHERING

329 Kedzie Avenue

Evanston, IL 60202

Home: 708-555-8487

E-mail: Gghering@xxx.com

OBJECTIVE

Obtain a position as an assistant advertising account executive

SKILLS & ACHIEVEMENTS

- Coordinated media planning and buying
- Researched potential markets for ad campaigns
- Supervised artwork, layout, and production
- Handled sales promotions
- Wrote original copy for ads
- Supervised trade shows and press shows
- Arranged and conducted sales meetings
- Wrote and distributed press releases
- Acted as liaison to outside ad agencies

WORK EXPERIENCE

Advertising Coordinator, 2000 - present
Scandinavian Design, Evanston, IL

Assistant Coordinator of Advertising, 1995 - 2000
Marshall Fields, Northbrook, IL

Assistant Sales Manager, 1993 - 1995
Rose Records, Skokie, IL

Sales Representative, 1991 - 1993
Gemco, Inc., Chicago, IL

EDUCATION

B.A. in English, Northwestern University, June 1991

SEMINARS

"Advertising 2001" - Northwestern University, 2001
"Account Management" - Loyola University, 2000

REFERENCES

Available on request

CAROLINE NOE

5311 W. Cerritos Blvd. • Bloomington, IN 48331
Carol.Noe@xxx.com • Home: (417) 555-9981

JOB OBJECTIVE

Obtain a position as a public relations director

ACCOMPLISHMENTS

- Served local community and civic organizations as part-time public relations representative
- Coordinated fund-raising
- Wrote successful grant proposals
- Gathered and assembled information for press releases
- Made appearances on local radio and TV programs
- Wrote copy for promotional programs
- Interacted successfully with public affairs representatives in local media

WORK HISTORY

Bloomington Press, Bloomington, IN
Advertising Assistant, 2000 to Present

St. Andrews Hospital, Bloomington, IN
Assistant Public Relations Director, 1998 to 2000

McKinney for Congress, Indianapolis, IN
Assistant Fund-Raising Coordinator, 1998

EDUCATION

University of Mississippi, Jackson, MS
B.A. in Communications, May 1998

SKILLS

- Proficient in Microsoft Word, Excel, PowerPoint, and Access
- Familiar with the A.P. Style Guide
- Extensive knowledge of local government, media, and community organizations

REFERENCES

On Request

CAROL BAKER

4420 Sunset Blvd. • Hollywood, CA 90027
Cellular: 213-555-9098 • C.Baker@xxx.com

JOB SOUGHT

Promotion director for a TV station

SKILLS AND ACHIEVEMENTS

Promotion/Marketing
- Wrote and designed promotional pieces
- Evaluated content and direction of promotions
- Handled market and demographic research
- Consulted clients on marketing plans

Video Production
- Handled shooting procedures, audio, lighting, casting, and editing
- Wrote and edited shooting scripts
- Determined production values for marketing accounts
- Oversaw postproduction and placement
- Coordinated presentations to clients

Media Planning
- Advised clients on media strategies
- Oversaw media budgets
- Determined and implemented marketing objectives
- Negotiated spot rates for clients

EMPLOYMENT HISTORY

Geary Advertising, Inc., Los Angeles, CA
Media Planner, 1994 to Present

Goebert & Radner, Inc., Chicago, IL
Assistant Media Buyer, 1991 to 1994

Sears Inc., Chicago, IL
Advertising Assistant, 1990 to 1991

EDUCATION

Drake University, Des Moines, IA
B.A. in Economics, Minor in Advertising, 1990, Phi Beta Kappa

Beverly Levine
1723 Lincoln Park West, #3B
Chicago, IL 60613
847/555-2332

CAREER OBJECTIVE   Arts writer/reporter for a newspaper

EXPERIENCE
- Wrote several articles for series "Chicago Lithographers" for *Chicago Artist* magazine.
- Wrote four in-depth feature articles for *Art Monthly.*
- Wrote and illustrated a children's series for Youth Press. Subjects included painting, music, film, and poetry.
- Reviewed books and film for *Lincoln Park Observer.*

EMPLOYMENT HISTORY

Freelance Writer, 2000 to Present

Youth Press, Wilmette, IL
Writer/Illustrator, 1996 to 1999

Art Monthly, San Francisco, CA
Staff Writer, 1993 to 1996

EDUCATION

Mills College, Oakland, CA
B.A. in English, 1993

Numerous workshops including:
- Express Yourself! Write in Your Voice
- Writing Techniques
- Short Story Workshop
- The Children's Perspective

REFERENCES AND WRITING SAMPLES AVAILABLE

Margaret Chapman

9484 N. Ellis Street   Home: 410/555-3949
Baltimore, MD 21203   Work: 410/555-5900 ext. 211

Overview

Ten years' experience as an editor and technical writer preparing publications and proposals for the scientific community. Extensive knowledge in production of books, academic journals, newsletters, brochures, EPA environmental impact reports, and permit applications. Proficient in numerous computer programs and capable of overseeing documents through all phases of development, from research to publication.

Skills

Technical Writing

- Preparation of EPA toxicology and pesticide reports for Actron Corporation
- Creation of environmental impact statements and sections of EPA reports to Congress for Bartlett Communications Group
- Development of newsletter articles on microelectronics and biomedical engineering for University of Maryland Publications Division
- Creation of criteria documents at American Environmental Health Inc. for submission to National Institute of Occupational Safety and Health

Editing

- Managing editor for *Journal of Modern Microbiology*. Solicit manuscripts, supervise peer review, hire and manage copyeditors and proofreaders, submit camera-ready copy to printer for quarterly scientific journal
- Copyeditor for numerous educational publications produced by University of Maryland.
- Edit and rewrite distance learning modules relating to the environmental impact of farming near urban communities for the U.S. Department of Agriculture

Page 1 of 2

Employment History

University of Maryland Publications Division
Managing Editor
Journal of Modern Microbiology
2000 to Present

University of Maryland Publications Division
Associate Editor of Educational Materials
1998 to 2000

Actron Corporation
Senior Technical Writer
1996 to 1998

Bartlett Communications Group
Technical Writer
1995 to 1996

American Environmental Health Inc.
Technical Communications Specialist
1993 to 1995

Education

B.S., University of Maryland, 1993
Double Major in English and Biology

References

References and writing samples are available on request

FRANK CARLSON

1500 THIRD STREET
NEW YORK, NY 10019
212/555-3994
WWW.FRANKCARLSONART.COM

GOAL

A position as an advertising agency art director

SKILLS & ACCOMPLISHMENTS

- Oversaw all artwork at advertising agency
- Hired artists, researchers, copywriters, and creative assistants
- Conferred with clients regarding advertising strategy
- Formulated design concepts
- Assigned work to artists, photographers, and writers
- Produced layouts and illustrations using PageMaker and Adobe software
- Researched market for products
- Conducted product comparison studies
- Wrote and edited copy for ads, flyers, and inserts
- Made sales presentations

WORK EXPERIENCE

Terrance Harris Agency, New York, NY
Senior Art Director, 1996 to Present
Staff Artist, 1994 to 1996

Carlson, Inc., San Francisco, CA
Freelance Commercial Artist, 1988 to 1994

Dandlor Corporation, Chicago, IL
Researcher/Copywriter, 1984 to 1988

EDUCATION

Boston University, Boston, MA
B.A. in Advertising, 1987

Art Institute of Chicago, Chicago, IL
Summer, 1986

JACK BISHOP

444 E. 17th Street • Cincinnati, OH 58278
J.Bishop@xxx.com • 513-555-2909

Goal

A career in television production

Accomplishments

Television Production
• Served as assistant producer for local daily news magazine
• Conducted interviews for stories
• Scouted locations for filming
• Supervised crew on location
• Researched and developed story concepts

Reporting
• Cultivated contacts
• Wrote human interest features
• Researched and produced features on local politics
• Conducted interviews

Film
• Edited videotape for local news magazine
• Edited videotape for promotional programs
• Filmed pieces for news show

Employment History

Gruber Productions, Cincinnati, OH
Creative Director, 1996 to Present

WCIN-TV, Cincinnati, OH
Producer, 1992 to 1996

KBLX Radio, San Francisco, CA
News Director, 1988 to 1992

Albuquerque News, Albuquerque, NM
Reporter, 1985 to 1988

Education

Duke University, Chapel Hill, NC
B.S. in Journalism, 1985

LISA HOLMES   *4226 Gleason Road*
Skokie, IL 60646
Lisa.Holmes@xxx.com
847-555-5858

OBJECTIVE

Opportunity for continued professional development and community service providing educational development services to a midsize nonprofit group.

EXPERIENCE

MIDWEST BOTANICAL GARDENS
Director, Educational Development Programs
September 1996 to Present
➤ Design and implement educational programs in the following areas: staff development, public school educational tours, garden club tours, and community outreach efforts.
➤ Implemented fundraising and grantwriting projects that increased department's budget by 15%.
➤ Increased benefactors' donations to the memorial garden by 10% last year.

WALKER SCIENCE MUSEUM
Manager, Children's Discovery Center
January 1992 to September 1996
➤ Supervised and enhanced visitor use of enclosed children's center within museum.
➤ Coordinated and supervised all special events.

EDUCATION

B.S. in Education, December 1991
Northern Illinois University
Minor in Botany

REFERENCES

Available on request

JUAN C. GARCIA

2103 Afton Street   Temple Hill, Maryland 20748   Home (301) 555-2419   Juan.Garcia@xxx.com

EDUCATION:

Columbia University, New York, NY
Majors: Communications, Business
– Degree expected: B.S., June 2003
– Grade point average: 3.7
– Regents Scholarship recipient
– Columbia University Scholarship recipient

EXPERIENCE:

7/01-Present   Graduate Business Library, Columbia University, NY
– Perform all general library duties
– Database management
– Sign out and catalog microfiche
– Reserve and distribute materials

9/00-5/01   German Department, Columbia University, NY
– Performed general office duties
– Offered extensive assistance by phone and in person
– Collated and proofread class materials
– Assisted professors in the gathering of class materials

6/00-9/00   Loan Collections Department, Columbia University, NY
– Initiated and completed new filing system for the office
– Checked arrears in Bursar's Office during registration period

9/99-5/00   School of Continuing Education, Columbia University, NY
– Involved in heavy public contact and problem solving
– General administrative duties

SPECIAL ABILITIES:

Fluent in Spanish
Currently studying German
BASIC programming skills
Proficient computer skills for all aspects of employment

REFERENCES:

Available on request

JEFFREY SCOTT ROHN

9229 E. Adler Drive • Wheaton, IL 60089
815/555-2621 (Office) • J.S.Rohn@xxx.com

OBJECTIVE

Editorial Assistant for Allstate Corporate Publications

ACCOMPLISHMENTS

Editing

- Redesigned *Discoveries*, a company publication, improving both content and visual appeal.
- Developed a database to maintain accurate mailing list.
- Supervised design and layout of publication.
- Improved quality of paper and photography.
- Reduced costs while increasing readership.
- Solicited feature articles from new writers.

Writing

- Researched, wrote, and edited articles for company publications.
- Wrote budget reports and grant proposals.
- Researched and wrote a report on software applications.
- Wrote a technical report on the feasibility of office copying systems.

EMPLOYMENT HISTORY

Allstate Insurance Company, Northbrook, IL
Editor, *Discoveries*, 1999 to Present
Graphic Designer, 1997 to 1999
Staff Artist, 1992 to 1997
Administrative Assistant, 1991 to 1992

EDUCATION

University of Wisconsin, Madison, WI
B.A. in Art, December 1990

SPECIAL SKILLS

- Fluent in Spanish
- Proficient in Microsoft Office Suite, PageMaker, and Adobe
- Familiar with the A.P. Style Guide

References Available on Request

DAVID GOTTNER

35666 Hialeah Ave. #6
Hialeah, FL 33333

Home: 305/555-2319
Work: 305/555-4700

Job Objective
Commercial artist for a major newspaper with the goal of media management.

Skills
- Illustration
- Layout
- Copywriting
- Research
- Photography

Accomplishments
- Designed and illustrated a literary journal.
- Served as artistic consultant for various university departments.
- Taught classes in commercial art at the college level including Principles of Layout, Line Drawing, Advertising, Copywriting, and Photography.

Employment History
Dade Community College, Miami, FL
Assistant Professor, Art Department
1997 to Present

Education
Northwestern University, Evanston, IL
M.A. in Fine Arts, 1996

Pinkens College, Fort Briggs, MO
B.A. in Art, 1985

References
Available

Shirley G. Botern

7 Pine Knoll Drive
Baltimore, MD 02293
301-555-5665
S.Botern@xxx.com

Career Goal: Bookstore Management

Overview:
- Extensive experience in retail sales and bookstore sales
- Supervisory background
- Excellent written and verbal communications skills
- Marketing and cash management experience
- Knowledge of Microsoft Word, Access, Excel, and PowerPoint
- Highly organized and creative professional able to develop creative marketing strategies, train employees, assist customers, and contribute to productive work environment

Work History: Manager, Sunshine Express (Children's Bookstore)
Baltimore, MD
1996 to Present

Assistant Manager, Fifth Street Books and Music
Chicago, IL
1992 to 1996

Salesperson, Necessary Things Gift Shop
Chicago, IL
1990 to 1992

Education: Northern Illinois University
Attended 1988 to 1990
Coursework in Business and Marketing

References: Available

CHRISTOPHER SCHMIDTT

65 Drake Street
St. Louis, MO 53190
Home: (314) 555-2222
Cellular: (314) 555-8700

JOB SOUGHT: Account Executive for Public Relations Firm

SKILLS & ACCOMPLISHMENTS:
◆ Handle public relations activities for seven clients
◆ Develop product and service publicity
◆ Write and edit press releases
◆ Purchase advertising space
◆ Schedule news conferences
◆ Supervise a staff of three writers
◆ Oversee budgets and expenses
◆ Plan and lead meetings
◆ Design graphics and layout

EMPLOYMENT HISTORY:

1995 to Present • Henry Stone Public Relations, St. Louis, MO
Public Relations Director

1991 to 1995 • Avenue Graphics, Chicago, IL
Graphic Artist

1984 to 1990 • Mark Shale, Skokie, IL
Salesperson

EDUCATION:

1983 Northeastern Illinois, Chicago, IL
B.A. in Biology

1990 to 1993 • Art Institute of Chicago, Chicago, IL
Graphic Arts Courses

• EUGENE T. SNOW

432 Sentinel Avenue • Kansas City, MO 74309 • 816-555-3903

• WORK HISTORY

1996 to Present
Staff Writer, *Consumer News*
Kansas City, MO

Write and edit feature articles. Develop story ideas. Author of the monthly feature "Best Buys." Conduct consumer interest polls, test consumer products, and report findings. Provide photography and perform photo research in support of articles. Participate in staff meetings to plan focus of each issue, determine magazine's short-term goals and long-range planning. Knowledge of A.P. style guidelines, attention to detail, and respect for deadlines.

1990 to 1996
Staff Writer, Children's Advocacy Network
St. Louis, MO

Produced monthly newsletter, brochures, press releases, feature articles, and speeches for nonprofit group dedicated to child welfare issues. Developed desktop publishing skills and ability to produce multimedia presentations. Knowledge of PageMaker, QuarkXPress, and PowerPoint.

• CREDENTIALS

June 1990
B.A. in English, Stevens College
G.P.A. of 3.8

May 1992
Winner, Scripps Prize for Excellence in Communications

REFERENCES AVAILABLE

Michael E. Marlow

4455 W. Gunderson • Berkley, CA 91404
415-555-4909 • M.Marlow@xxx.com

Job Sought

A position in an advertising agency where I can utilize my graphic design skills.

Education

University of California at Berkeley, Berkeley, CA
B.A. in Visual Communications; degree expected, June 2002

Areas of concentration include: Graphic Design, Typography, Lettering, Package Design, Illustration, Photography, Calligraphy, and Industrial Technology.

Work Experience

What's Hip Advertising, Inc., San Francisco, CA
Staff Artist, Summer 2000, 2001

- Handled concept development, design and layout, typesetting, and placement of ads for agency.
- Assisted in-house design staff with computer illustration and layout using Adobe software.

Strange's Art Supplies, Berkeley, CA
Sales Assistant, Part-Time, 1999 - present

- Assist students, artists, and designers with choosing art supplies.
- Handle cash deposits and credit card transactions.
- Train new employees.

Honors

Earth Day Poster Competition, Honorable Mention, 2001
Berkeley Chamber of Commerce Design Show, Second Place, 2000
American Society of Magazine Designers Scholarship, 1999

Activities

Berkeley Design Club, Secretary, 2000 - present
Designers in Progress, Member, 1999 - present
Gambols Poster Design Workshop, Wichita, KS, 2000

References

Provided on request

■ ■ ■ **Martin T. Scott**

343 Evansville Avenue   **MTScott@xxx.com**
Albany, New York 12908   **(518) 555-2902**

■ **Objective:**   Public Relations Representative

■ **Skills:**   Media Relations
                        Crisis Containment
                        Community Relations
                        Television Relations and Production
                        Community Activism
                        Research, Writing, and Editing
                        Speechwriting
                        Desktop Publishing
                        Photography and Layout

■ **Experience:**   **6/97 - Present**
                        Public Relations Coordinator
                        Citizen's Action Network, Albany

                        ■ Handle all public relations activities.
                        ■ Write and edit press releases and speeches.
                        ■ Schedule news conferences.
                        ■ Direct production of newsletter and direct mail pieces.
                        ■ Supervise staff of three writers and two graphic artists.

                        6/94 - 6/97
                        Public Relations Director
                        ALERT, Chicago

                        ■ Developed and produced media projects including feature
                          articles, public service announcements, and educational
                          video related to special education.
                        ■ Responsible for multimedia presentations to educational,
                          community, and parent support groups nationwide.

Page 1 of 2

■ **Experience:**   **8/90 - 6/94**
(continued)   *Writer*
                    Harrison Communications, Philadelphia

■ Produced public service announcements for radio and television.
■ Designed and wrote brochures, posters, and direct mail pieces for wide range of clients including public libraries, hospitals, nonprofit groups, and professional associations.
■ Extensive experience developing educational and health care support materials.

■ **Education:**   May 1990
                   B.A. in Marketing
                   Minor in English
                   Northwestern University, Evanston, IL

■ **Memberships:**   1992 - Present
                     American Marketing Association

                     1993 - Present
                     Public Relations Society of America Inc.

■ **References:**   References and portfolio are available.

CARLOS VEGA

548 W. Hollywood Way

Burbank, CA 91505

c.vega@xxx.com

818/555-9090

Professional Objective

An upper-level management position in the recording industry where I can employ my promotion and marketing experience.

Professional Background

Warner Brothers Records, Burbank, CA
Director of Marketing/Jazz Department, 1996 to Present

➤ Develop and maintain strategic marketing campaigns for new releases and catalog.
➤ Produce reissue packages and samplers, both retail and promotional.
➤ Create ad copy.
➤ Interface with creative services and national and local print and radio.
➤ Oversee all aspects of sales.
➤ Coordinate promotional activities and chart reports.

I.R.S. Records, Los Angeles, CA
National Sales Manager, 1992 to 1996
West Coast Sales Manager, 1989 to 1992

➤ Increased sales profile, specifically West Coast retailers, one-stops, and racks.
➤ Promoted to national sales manager, where I established sales and promotion programs for the company.
➤ Coordinated radio/chart reports.

Page 1 of 2

Professional Background *(continued)*

Specialty Records, Scranton, PA
Sales Representative, 1988

➤ Handled sales, merchandising, and account servicing for LPs and cassettes.
➤ Called on major chains and small independent retailers.
➤ Promoted new releases and maintained account inventory.

Tower Records, Los Angeles, CA
Manager, 1987 to 1988

➤ Handled sales, merchandising, and customer service.
➤ Product selection and ordering.
➤ Personnel management and supervision for a full-time retail outfit.

MCA Records Distribution, Universal City, CA
Sales Representative, 1981 to 1987

➤ Promoted and sold MCA product in Los Angeles and surrounding counties.
➤ Designed in-store and window displays.
➤ Coordinated media advertising support programs.

Education

Berkeley University, Berkeley, CA
B.A., Liberal Arts, 1981

References Available

LINDA MAXWELL

916 Rockport Road • Phoenix, AZ 85016
602-555-6868 (evenings)
602-555-9136 (days)
www.maxit.com

OBJECTIVE

To obtain a position as a marketing executive

WORK HISTORY

9/00 to Present
Marketing Manager
Southwest Publishing, Phoenix

Duties include:
- Direct publisher's marketing efforts
- Produce catalogs and direct mail pieces
- Coordinate with advertising department
- Track sales histories and design pricing and promotional strategies.
- Hire, train, and supervise sales staff
- Represent publisher at sales conventions and industry trade shows
- Liaison to wholesalers and distributors

5/97 to 8/00
Advertising Copywriter
Current Communications, Inc., Phoenix

Duties included:
- Produced ad copy and brochures
- Designed, produced, and distributed direct mail packages
- Product research

6/96 to 5/97
Telemarketer
TDK Marketing, Dallas

Duties included:
- Conducted phone surveys to research consumer preferences and purchase patterns.
- Compiled results and drafted reports.

Page 1 of 2

EDUCATION

B.S. in Communications
University of Arizona
June 1996

MEMBERSHIPS

American Marketing Association
National Association of Women in Business

REFERENCES

Portfolio and complete list of references supplied on request.

Christopher Knight

1700 W. Armadillo
San Diego, CA 90087
619/555-9000
619/555-2839

Objective

To obtain a position as vice-president of public relations with an aeronautical corporation.

Areas of Experience

Marketing Development
- Initiated and supervised sales programs for aircraft distributors selling aircraft to businesses throughout the western United States.
- Managed accounts with a profit range of $100,000 to $1,000,000, including Dow Chemical, Landston Steel, Mercury Co., Berkley Metallurgical, and Ford Motor Co.
- Demonstrated to customer companies how to use aircraft to coordinate and consolidate expanding facilities.
- Introduced and expanded use of aircraft for musical tours.

Public Relations
- Handled all levels of sales promotion, corporate public relations, and training of industry on company use of aircraft.
- Managed promotion including personal presentations, radio and TV broadcasts, news stories, and magazine features.

Pilot Training
- Taught primary, secondary, and instrument flight in single and multi-engine aircraft.

Employment History

Hughes Aircraft, Inc., San Diego, CA
Sales Manager and Chief Pilot
1991 to Present

Boeing Corporation, Kansas City, MO
Assistant Manager of Promotion
1982 to 1990

American Airlines, Dallas, TX
Pilot
1975 to 1982

United States Air Force, Houston, TX
Flight Instructor
1973 to 1975

Professional License

Airline Transport Rating 14352-60
Single, Multi-Engine Land
Flight Instructor - Instrument

Education

University of Texas, Austin, TX
B.A. in History, 1961

Military Service

United States Air Force
1973 to 1975

References

Available on request

Renee Glykison

8 E. Western Avenue • Houston, TX 75737 • 713/555-8098

Job Objective

To obtain a position as an assistant sales manager at a publishing company.

Achievements

- Orchestrated market analyses and researched competition for reports to the district manager.
- Identified clients' needs and problems and assured them of personal attention.
- Prepared sales forecasts and sales goals reports.
- Resolved service and billing problems.
- Developed monthly sales plans to identify necessary account maintenance and specific problems that required attention.
- Delivered sales presentations to groups and individuals.
- Maintained daily sales logs and referral logs.
- Identified potential new clients and established new accounts.
- Increased client base by 50 percent.

Employment History

American National Books, Inc., Houston, TX
Assistant Manager, 2000 to Present

Unico International, Dallas, TX
Sales Representative, 1997 to 2000

Midwest Books, Omaha, NE
Salesperson, 1996 to 1997

Education

Austin College, Austin, TX
B.A. in History, 1992

References Available

KEVIN WINTERS

5440 Magnolia Way #43 • Savannah, GA 30209 • 912/555-3930

OBJECTIVE: Full-time, in-house position as book editor

WORK HISTORY:
8/93 to Present   *Freelance Editor*
Clients:
- Creative Publishing Inc.
- University of Georgia
- Peterson Press
- National Educational Institute
- Dade Publications Ltd.

Provide project management and editing services to book publishers. Experienced in developmental and content editing, as well as copyediting.

Accomplishments:
- Wrote tests and other supplemental materials for National Educational Institute.
- Developed format and author instructions for new line of cookbooks for Creative Publishing Inc.
- Supervised photo research for several four-color textbooks.
- Americanized British travel guides for use in the U.S.

8/89 to 8/93   *Editor*, **Creative Publishing, Atlanta, GA**
- Series editor in charge of cookbook and craft book line.
- Did all acquisitions and production management of line.
- Supervised two in-house editors and one editorial assistant.
- Coordinated all details of production with authors, editors, designers, and marketing staff.
- Represented the line at conventions.

5/85 to 8/89   *Assistant Editor*, **Technical Guides Inc., Atlanta, GA**
- Copyeditor for small publisher specializing in home repair and building manuals.

CREDENTIALS:
5/85   B.A. in English, University of Georgia
Member   American Publishing Association

SUSAN K. WORTH

492 PRATT AVENUE
HUNTINGTON VALLEY, PA 19006
(215) 555-9711
S.WORTH@XXX.COM

GOAL: Public Relations Specialist

EMPLOYMENT:

2000 to Present
Community Liaison
Huntington Animal Shelter

- Design and administer programs to increase public awareness of shelter and animal welfare issues.
- Responsible for weekly cable TV show explaining pet care.
- Administer and publicize Adopt-A-Pet events.
- Participate in fund-raising events.

1999 to 2000
Assistant Director of Community Relations
Huntington General Hospital

- Assisted director with all aspects of community relations, including fund-raising events and off-site presentations to schools and community groups.
- Assisted with writing of newsletter and press releases.
- Assisted with production of Health TV shows (community access programming).

1997 to 1999
Marketing Representative
Creative Greetings, Inc.

- Local representative for national greeting card chain.
- Represented manufacturer to local stores.
- Negotiated for shelf space.
- Maintained inventory.

Page 1 of 2

EMPLOYMENT:
(CONTINUED)

1995 to 1997
Office Manager
Plankton Street Pet Clinic (Austin, TX)

- Responsible for all aspects of office management.
- Clerical, accounting, and receptionist duties.
- Assisted vets with routine care of animals in the boarding kennel.

EDUCATION:

Austin College, Austin, TX
B.A. in Marketing
June 1997

REFERENCES:

On request

PETER GILBERT DUFFY

553 S. Cicero Avenue
Chicago, IL 60622
312-555-5999

GOAL
To obtain a professional copywriting position that utilizes my knowledge of fashion marketing.

ASSETS
- Strong sense of color and design
- Excellent written and oral communication skills
- Self-directed and deadline-oriented
- Team player
- Computer literate

ACHIEVEMENTS
- Produced advertising copy for four major ad campaigns: Best Jeans, Ms. Boutiques, Outdoor Gear, and Z-Sports.
- Wrote script for radio ad campaign for Z-Sports.
- Wrote copy for Outdoor Gear catalog and direct mail campaign.

EMPLOYMENT HISTORY
6/98 to Present   Senior Copywriter, Lee & Perkins Ad Inc.

3/96 to 6/98   Copywriter, Midwest Retailers Association

7/94 to 2/96   Editorial Assistant, *Chicago Style Magazine*

EDUCATION
Northwestern University, Evanston, IL
Bachelor of Arts with Honors in English, June 1994

School of the Art Institute
Coursework in Design, 1994 to 1996

Clarence Scott Talley

600 Porter St. • **Las Vegas, NV 89890** • **702/555-3893** • **cst@xxx.com**

Education

University of Nevada, Las Vegas, NV
Bachelor of Arts in Communications
Expected June 2002

Honors

Dean's List (four semesters)
Dornburn Academic Merit Scholarship
U.N.L.V. Communications Award (given to outstanding student researcher)

Activities

President, Kappa Beta Fraternity
New Student Week Committee
Homecoming Planning Committee
Captain, Tennis Team

Work Experience

Porter & Rand Associates, Seattle, WA
Advertising Intern, 2001
Assisted sales staff in the areas of research, demographics,
sales forecasts, identifying new customers, and promotion.

University of Nevada, Las Vegas, NV
Research/Office Assistant, 2000-2001
Researched and compiled materials for department professors.
Arranged filing system and supervisor's library.
Organized department inventory.

Skills

Strong computer background.
Experience in research including library, government, and online resources.
Adept at writing, editing, and design.

YOORI MATSUKA

Fulton Hall • 2300 East Harrison, Rm 306 • Chicago, IL 60633
312/555-4849 • ymatsuka@xxx.com

OBJECTIVE: A career in international communications.

EDUCATION: University of Illinois at Chicago, Chicago, IL
                      Bachelor of Arts in Communications
                      Expected June 2003

HONORS: Phi Beta Kappa
                      Dean's list five times
                      Robeson Communications Scholarship, 2002

ACTIVITIES: Vice President, Gamma Fraternity
                      Freshman Advisor
                      Homecoming Planning Committee
                      Baseball Team
                      Student Rights Group

WORK EXPERIENCE: **P.R. Intern, 2002**
                      Westbrook Theater, Chicago, IL
                      • Wrote and edited press releases and public service
                        announcements.
                      • Developed relationships with local columnists.
                      • Wrote ad copy for print and radio media.

                      Office Assistant, Journalism School, 2000
                      University of Illinois at Chicago
                      • Assisted with registrations, filing, and typing.
                      • Arranged application materials.
                      • Assembled course packs.

                      General Office, Registrar, 1999-2000
                      • Processed transcript requests.
                      • Entered registrations on the computer.
                      • Provided assistance to students.

SPECIAL SKILLS: Strong computer background
                      Fluent in Japanese
                      Understanding of international relations and cultural differences

REFERENCES: Available on request.

RHONDA WARONKER

5320 Wilshire Blvd.   Los Angeles, CA 90069   213/555-9282

OBJECTIVE

Seeking a publicity/marketing position in the communications industry.

WORK EXPERIENCE

WRT Records, Los Angeles, CA
Marketing Director, 9/00-present
- Handle distribution, retail marketing, advertising, and mail order marketing.
- Write biographies and coordinate publicity.
- Obtain knowledge regarding domestic and overseas independent distribution, buyers for U.S. chain stores, and *Billboard* reporters.

Hit Productions, Los Angeles, CA
Public Relations/Marketing Assistant, 5/99-9/00
- Assisted PR Director with all duties, including radio promotion and retail marketing.
- Coordinated radio and print interviews for artists.
- Typing, filing, and answering phones.

KTWV Radio, Los Angeles, CA
Music Director, 6/98-5/99
- Selected appropriate music for a contemporary jazz format.
- Oversaw daily operations of music library and programming department.
- Supervised a staff of six.

EDUCATION

UCLA, Los Angeles, CA
B.A. in Arts Management, June 1998

ACTIVITIES

Phi Mu Alpha Music Fraternity, President
National Association of College Activities
Alpha Lambda Fraternity

SKILLS

Working knowledge of Microsoft Office and Lotus.

SANDRA L. PEARSON

12 E. Tenth Street
San Francisco, CA 98490
Home: 415-555-2343
sandy.pearson@xxx.com

JOB OBJECTIVE
A management position in cable television advertising sales.

RELEVANT EXPERIENCE
- Sold space in television for four major clients in the automotive industry.
- Served as liaison between clients and television and radio station salespeople.
- Researched demographic and public buying habits for clients.
- Sold space for daytime programming on local TV station.
- Advised station on content and suitability of ads.
- Served as liaison between station and those purchasing advertising space.

EMPLOYMENT HISTORY
Medialink Advertising Agency, San Francisco, CA
Television Space Sales, September 1995 - Present

KTUT Television, Portland, OR
Television Space Sales, October 1993 - August 1995

KFTF Radio, Berkley, CA
Staff Sales Assistant, June 1991 - June 1993

EDUCATION
B.A. in Communications, University of California at Berkeley, June 1993

HONORS
- Seeger Award, Outstanding Communications Senior, 1993
- Dean's List, five semesters

Page 1 of 2

REFERENCES

Martin K. Smith, Vice President of Sales
Medialink
4339 Garrett Parkway
San Francisco, CA 98490
415/555-4948 Ext. 388
Msmith@xxx.com

Elizabeth Conway, Former Director of Sales at Medialink
Marketing Manager
Superior Package Systems
558 W. Sutton Road
Brooklyn, NY 12909
718/555-3977
E.Conway@xxx.com

Robert Fulton
KTUT Television
Sales Manager
883 E. Grand Street
Portland, OR 76881
322/555-2914
Bob.Fulton@xxx.com

Samantha T. Shavers

15 E. Green Street #333
Richmond, VA 18978
Sam.Shavers@xxx.com
(804)555-3903

OVERVIEW

Experienced technical writer capable of producing quality materials such as:
• product proposals
• advertising and catalog copy
• technical manuals
• scientific research proposals
• documentation for software systems
• environmental impact statements

CLIENTS

• Jenkins Manufacturing, Richmond, VA
• Cooper Technical Publications, Atlanta, GA
• Electronic Design Inc., Richmond, VA
• Jones & Wright Environmental Inc., Washington, DC
• Software Solutions Inc., Atlanta, GA

CREDENTIALS

B.A. in English, University of Wisconsin
June 2001
Minor: Computer Science

Member, Society for Technical Communications

REFERENCES

References and writing samples available

Wilard Paddock

343 S. Park Street
Washington, DC 02221
202/555-3247

Job Objective: Art Director

Work Experience: Umbrella Advertising, Inc., Washington, DC
Senior Art Director, 1993-Present
Staff Artist, 1990-1992
▼ Oversee production of all artwork.
▼ Responsible for hiring artists, researchers, copywriters, and creative assistants.
▼ Coordinate with clients regarding advertising strategy.
▼ Formulate design concepts.
▼ Assign work to artists, photographers, and writers.

Artworks, Inc., Scranton, PA
Freelance Commercial Artist, 1984-1990
▼ Produced general board work, illustrations, layouts, and mechanicals for a department store chain and several ad agencies.

Parker & Parker, Inc., Chicago, IL
Researcher/Copywriter, 1980-1984
▼ Researched market products.
▼ Conducted comparison studies with other products.
▼ Devised concepts for ads.
▼ Wrote copy for ads, flyers, and inserts.
▼ Developed sales presentations.

Education: Penn State University, Allentown, PA
B.A. in Advertising, 1980

Inglewood School of Design, Inglewood, CA
Summer 1980

References: Available upon request

SHARON KLEINBACH
9000 Inez Drive
Tacoma, WA 98899
s.kleinbach@xxx.com
206-555-2909

JOB OBJECTIVE
Assistant Director of Public Relations

SKILLS & ACCOMPLISHMENTS
Public Relations
- Prepared news releases.
- Maintained personal media contacts.
- Prepared and edited copy for brochures.
- Helped to develop advertising plans.
- Edited copy for newsletter.
- Prepared and distributed newsletter to patrons.
- Handled all booking for live entertainment.

Office Management
- Coordinated workshops and seminars on publicity.
- Handled group travel and hotel arrangements.
- Supervised an office staff of eight.
- Maintained business calendar.
- Organized staff meetings.
- Booked convention space.
- Prepared financial reports.

EMPLOYMENT HISTORY
Park America, Tacoma, WA
Administrative Assistant to Director of Public Relations,
1996 to Present

Office Manager, 1993 to 1996

EDUCATION

Brooklyn College, Brooklyn, NY
B.A. in English Literature, June 1993

SPECIAL SKILLS

Typing Speed: 60 wpm
Dictation
Word Processing
Knowledge of Microsoft Office 2000

REFERENCES

Available on request

REBECCA MORNEY

4440 E. 14th Street • Bronx, NY 10009 • B.Morney@xxx.com • 212/555-1298

Goal

Recreational Director

Overview

Extensive experience designing activities programs for all age groups.
Able to meet needs of diverse client base while offering:
- Strong writing and communication skills
- Knowledge of Spanish and Italian
- Guitar and piano skills
- Drawing ability

Experience

Director, After School Programs
District 219
June 1999 to Present

Program Director
Bronx Community Center
May 1996 to June 1999

Director of Activities
Carlson College
September 1994 to May 1996

Credentials

B.A. in Recreational Studies
Northern Illinois University, DeKalb, IL
May 1994

References

Available

RICK MARTINEZ

5895 E. Friar Road
Bronx, NY 10009
212-555-4998

OBJECTIVE

Advertising Production

WORK EXPERIENCE

1999 - Present
Broadway Magazine, **New York, NY**
Assistant Production Manager

- Direct all aspects of production and printing for national publication.
- Heavy client and agency contact.
- Organize and approve all art, layouts, and final films.
- Responsible for all in-depth contact with other media.
- Produce copy for ads.

1995 - 1999
Crazy Al's, Brooklyn, NY
Assistant to Promotion Manager

- Conducted all in-store promotions and publicity events.
- Placed advertising and publicity in local publications.
- Consulted on grand opening of Santa Monica store.
- Provided product information and direct assistance to consumers.

EDUCATION

University of Illinois, Champaign-Urbana, IL
B.S. in Marketing, December 1994

HONORS

Dean's List, 1994
Dirk Toomey Scholarship, 1993 and 1994

REFERENCES

Available on request.

RUTH M. DAVID
572 First Street • Brooklyn, NY 11215 • (212) 555-4328 • R.David@xxx.com

Education
Princeton University, Princeton, NJ
   Degree Expected: M.S. in Communications, June 2003
   Class Rank: Top ten percent
   Editor of *Communications Journal*

University of Wisconsin, Madison, WI
   B.A. in Political Science, May 2001
   Dean's List
   Marching Band Section Leader

Work History
Boston Theatre Co., Boston, MA
P.R. Internship, June 2002 to September 2002
   Composed press releases and public service announcements that publicized theatre
   events. Oversaw production of posters, flyers, and programs. Sold subscriptions and
   advertising space.

Other Experience
Citizens Action Group, New York, NY
Field Manager, June 2001 to September 2001
   Promoted public awareness of state legislative process and issues of toxic waste,
   utility control, and consumer legislation. Demonstrated effective fund-raising skills.

University of Wisconsin, Madison, WI
Resident Assistant, Residential Life Office, September 2000 to June 2001
   Administered all aspects of student affairs in university residence halls, including
   program planning, discipline, and individual and group counseling. Directed
   achievement of student goals through guidance of the residence hall council.
   Implemented all university policies.

University of Wisconsin, Madison, WI
Staff Training Lecturer, August 2000 to December 2000
   Conducted workshops for residence hall staff on counseling, effective
   communication, and conflict resolution.

Special Skills
Strong computer background
Knowledge of Spanish and French
CPR certified

References
Available on request.

DAVID THOMAS STIN

1001 W. Edina Avenue
Edina, MN 53989
Home: 612-555-5453
www.davidstin.com

CAREER OBJECTIVE

A challenging position as an artist for a small to midsize advertising agency.

EDUCATION

University of Minnesota, St. Paul, MN
B.A. in Commercial Art, expected June 2003

WORK EXPERIENCE

***Minneapolis Magazine*, Minneapolis, MN**
Commercial Artist, Summers 1999 - Present
• Produced line drawings for magazine ads, slides, and promotional materials.
• Gained experience in watercolors and acrylics.

University of Minnesota, St. Paul, MN
Designer, University Publications, 2001
• Handled all aspects of production from layout to finished product.
• Familiar with Adobe software systems.

University of Minnesota, St. Paul, MN
Photographer, *U.M. News*, 1999 - 2001
• Took photos for university newspaper.
• Assisted with placement and layout.

WORKSHOPS

Illustration Workshop, Art Institute of Chicago, 2000
Midwest Design Seminar, St. Paul, MN, 1999

W I N O N A   T .   S I M P S O N

420 W. Easterly Avenue   Home: 317/555-1267
Indianapolis, IN 49091   w.simpson@xxx.com

OBJECTIVE
A management position in marketing or public relations.

PROFESSIONAL ACHIEVEMENTS
Marketing/Public Relations
- Developed a successful marketing campaign for a video rental chain.
- Initiated and maintained a positive working relationship with radio and print media.
- Implemented marketing strategies to increase sales at less profitable stores.
- Designed a training program for store managers and staff.

Promotion
- Demonstrated electronic equipment in stereo and department stores.
- Reported customer reactions to manufacturers.
- Designed fliers and advertising to promote products.

EMPLOYMENT HISTORY
Blockbuster Video, Inc., Indianapolis, IN
P.R. Director, 1990-Present

Jeron Stereo, Bloomington, IN
Marketing Representative, 1987-1990

Kader Advertising, St. Louis, MO
P.R. Assistant, 1985-1987

EDUCATION
Washington University, St. Louis, MO
B.S. in Education, 1985

HONORS
Phi Beta Kappa, 1985
Top 5% of class
Dean's List

ANNA D. IMMEN

7009 Pinotta Drive South
Duluth, MN 61119
218/555-8393 (Day)
218/555-3839 (Evening)

OBJECTIVE

To obtain a position as a copywriter for a full-service publishing company.

EXPERIENCE

Timber Publishing, Inc., Duluth, MN
Staff Copywriter, 2000 - Present
- Created advertising copy for company's book catalogs.
- Composed jacket copy for books and captions for illustrations and sidebars.
- Handled layout and production.
- Edited and rewrote manuscripts in preparation for publication.

Anna D. Immen, Inc., Madison, WI
Freelance Writer, 1996 - 2000
- Edited five technical manuals on computer software.
- Scripted four industrial films for various food service companies.
- Developed two book ideas and drafted sales proposals for a book-packaging company.
- Composed copy for department store catalog.

EDUCATION

University of Wisconsin, Madison, WI
B.A. in English, 1996

HONORS

Phi Beta Kappa, 1996
Dean's List, 1995, 1996
Thomas Trumble Writing Competition, Second Prize, 1995

REFERENCES AVAILABLE

RUBIETTA WASHINGTON

453 Franklin Avenue   San Diego, CA 94890   (619) 555-3489

OBJECTIVE
A management position in public relations

WORK EXPERIENCE
JUST PASTA INC., San Diego, CA
Marketing Director, 1996 - present
- Developed a successful marketing campaign for a restaurant chain.
- Initiated and maintained a positive working relationship with radio and print media.
- Implemented marketing strategies to increase sales at least profitable outlets.
- Designed a training program for store managers and staff.

GREAT IDEAS CARPET CLEANING CO., Dallas, TX
Marketing Representative, 1992 - 1996
- Demonstrated carpet cleaners in specialty and department stores.
- Reported customer reactions to manufacturers.
- Designed fliers and advertising to promote products.
- Made frequent calls to retail outlets.

REBO CHIPS, INC., Chicago, IL
Assistant to Sales Manager, 1987 - 1992
- Handled both internal and external areas of sales and marketing, including samples, advertising, and pricing.
- Served as company sales representative and sold snack foods to retail outlets.

EDUCATION
UNIVERSITY OF ILLINOIS AT CHICAGO, Chicago, IL
B.A. Marketing, 1986

SEMINARS
San Diego State Marketing Workshop, 1996, 1997
Sales and Marketing Association Seminars, 1994

References available on request.

Chapter 6

Sample Cover Letters

This chapter contains many sample cover letters for people pursuing a wide variety of jobs and careers in the field of communication, or who have had experience in this field in the past.

There are many different styles of cover letters in terms of layout, level of formality, and presentation of information. These samples also represent people with varying amounts of education and work experience. Choose one cover letter or borrow elements from several different cover letters to help you construct your own.

Terri Franks
15 Nob Hill
San Francisco, CA 91405
415/555-4398

October 10, 20--

Gilbert Secor, President
Unicorn Design, Inc.
2442 Market Street, Suite 4C
San Francisco, CA 91407

Dear Mr. Secor:

I am interested in applying for the position of graphic designer that recently opened up in your company. I have enclosed my resume, and you will find that I possess the skills Unicorn Design is requesting.

I am a recent graduate of the Berkeley College of Design, where I received a B.A. in Graphic Design. My areas of concentration included photography, publication design, copywriting, typography, and packaging. I also have a B.A. in History from the University of Minnesota.

My experience includes the designing of ads, brochures, and posters for local organizations such as the Rotary Club, MADD, and Northview High School. I have also coordinated fashion shows and created various business systems. In addition, I have worked as a graphic design intern at Berkeley and as a graphics assistant at Fern Labs in Palo Alto.

After several years as a homemaker and mother, I have decided to pursue the design field. Now that I have earned my degree and gained the needed experience, I am ready for the challenge of a position at a company such as yours.

I would like to have the opportunity to show you my portfolio. Thank you for your consideration. I look forward to hearing from you.

Sincerely,

Terri Franks

MICHAEL ERVIN MCDONALD

333 E. RHETT DRIVE • AUGUSTA, GA 33390
404-555-0393 • M.E.MCDONALD@XXX.COM

October 26, 20--

KKBT Radio
5600 Sunset Blvd.
Los Angeles, CA 90028
Attn: Liz Kiley, Operations Manager

Dear Ms. Kiley:

This letter is in response to your ad in *Radio and Records* for a program director. I've been paying close attention to your station's recent changes in programming and was excited to hear that you have gone urban.

I have had extensive experience in the world of radio over the past fifteen years. I have served in a variety of capacities, including program director/music director at WROB in Robinson, IL; producer/announcer at WGAU in Augusta, GA; and producer/announcer for WREE in East St. Louis, IL. I am a graduate of the Midwest School of Broadcasting. Though my background has been in small radio markets, I feel I am ready to break into a major market.

Enclosed, you will find my resume. I am confident that my skills will fit the needs of KKBT and I would be an appropriate fit as the program director. I look forward to speaking with you in person.

Thank you for your time and consideration.

Sincerely,

Michael Ervin McDonald

MARTHA WAYANS
4500 W. 77th St.
New York, NY 10032
212/555-3839

August 28, 20--

George Jacobs
Human Resources
AT&T
1200 E. 5th Ave.
New York, NY 10019

Dear Mr. Jacobs:

Michelle Sanderson, who works in the sales department at AT&T, suggested
that I contact you regarding a possible opening in your public relations
department. I am enclosing my resume for your consideration.

I will be graduating this month from New York University with a degree in
Communications. My recent induction into the Communications Honor
Society (Beta Alpha Psi) was a personal milestone. I am also currently
a member of the Association of International Business (A.I.B.).

I am interested in working for the communications industry in the field of
public relations, and I feel that the best place for me to start would be at
AT&T.

I have enclosed my resume and will be calling you in about a week
to follow up on this letter. Please feel free to call Mrs. Sanderson for
a reference. Thank you for your time and consideration.

Sincerely,

Martha Wayans

Clarence Scott Talley

600 Porter St. • Las Vegas, NV 89890 • 702/555-3893 • cst@xxx.com

May 15, 20--

Mr. Tarskett Renu
Creative Director
Quest Advertising
2330 W. Delaney Blvd.
Los Angeles, CA 90029

Dear Mr. Renu:

I am inquiring as to whether there are any openings in your agency at the present time. Upon researching Quest Advertising, I became interested in the progressive and artistic environment your company has to offer.

I expect to graduate next month from the University of Nevada with a B.A. in Communications, and I am looking forward to a career in advertising. While at Nevada, I was awarded the Dornburn Scholarship and the Excellence in Communications Award. I have also made the Dean's List four times.

Last summer, I gained experience in the field by serving as an advertising intern for Porter and Rand Associates. At Porter and Rand, I assisted the sales staff in the areas of research, demographics, sales forecasts, and special promotions. The experience I gained throughout my education and during my internship has given me a strong foundation to begin my career in advertising.

I would appreciate hearing of any current openings at Quest, and I am willing to travel to Los Angeles at your convenience to discuss opportunities in person. Thank you for your consideration.

Sincerely,

Clarence Scott Talley

Marlene Drake
3300 Bay Road
Green Bay, WI 55390
414/555-4930

October 28, 20--

Derek Nord
NBC
Manager, Wardrobe Department
3300 Alamedia Drive
Burbank, CA 91505

Dear Mr. Nord:

I will be relocating to Los Angeles in late November and I'm hoping to explore job opportunities upon receiving my Master's in Theater Arts.

As you can see from my enclosed resume, I have extensive wardrobe experience. I worked for WWGB-TV as a wardrobe mistress and have handled the wardrobe for several bands in the Green Bay area. I have also had extensive experience with wardrobe in film and video.

I would like to meet with you while I am in town the week of November 5th to discuss any possible openings you may have in your wardrobe department. Please take a moment to review the enclosed resume, and I will contact you to arrange a time to meet.

Sincerely,

Marlene Drake

November 1, 20--

Mr. Peter Sauers
Managing Director
Sauers Productions, Inc.
550 Magnolia Way
Burbank, CA 91501

Dear Mr. Sauers:

This letter is to inquire about the possibility of an opening in your production company for a production assistant.

I have spent the last year working in Miami for New Order Productions as a production assistant. I have benefited greatly from this experience, but it has always been my dream to work in the Hollywood film industry. I recently received my B.A. in film production from the University of Florida. Last summer, I served as a production coordinator for Tert Films in Chicago; the previous summer I served as a production assistant for the Baltimore Film Festival.

It is my long-term goal to become a director of films, and I feel that a position with your company would be an excellent opportunity for me to learn and grow.

I will follow up this letter with a phone call early next week. Thank you for your time, and I look forward to meeting with you.

Sincerely,

Milton Carl Chapman

66446 Collins Avenue #4B
Miami, FL 30309
Home: 305/555-2930
Cellular: 303/555-2992

HARRISON CRUMB

3338 W. Redbook Drive   Home: (806) 555-1910
Amarillo, TX 78077   Pager: (806) 555-7730

January 2, 20--

Miles Franks
Director of Human Resources
WWTD-TV
4440 Peach Tree Avenue
Dallas, TX 78229

Dear Mr. Franks:

A mutual friend, Terrence Weber, informed me that you are looking for
a new Director of Traffic for your TV station. I have enclosed my resume,
and I am interested in applying for the position.

As Assistant Director of Traffic at WRMC-TV in Amarillo, I have acted
as the contact between syndication companies and the station, created
logos, established sales availabilities, and screened and processed
tapes and films. Previous to my tenure at WRMC-TV, I held the same
position at WPIX-TV in El Paso, where I was promoted from Assistant
to Head Programmer.

I believe that my seven years' experience well qualifies me for the next
logical step in my career: Director of Traffic. I would be happy to meet
with you at any time. Please contact me at your earliest convenience.

Sincerely,

Harrison Crumb

April 23, 20--

Rupert Goebert
Director
Santa Barbara Art Fair
6660 Forest Green Ave.
Santa Barbara, CA 92299

Dear Mr. Goebert:

I am interested in applying for the position of photographer for this year's Santa Barbara Art Fair. I recently learned of the open position from your posting at the civic center.

My photography experience includes a stint last year as official photographer for the Nevada State Fair, where I headed a team of photographers. I work with 35 mm and 2¼ x 2¼ inch cameras as well as video equipment. I have also photographed for products, promotions, press releases, and publications. I believe that my previous experience would enable me to do an excellent job for you.

I am a graduate of the University of Washington in Tacoma, where I earned a degree in Graphic Arts with a minor in Photography. I also have extensive experience as a graphic designer.

I have enclosed a copy of my resume and a few samples of my photography. I will be in touch with you next week regarding this letter.

Sincerely,

Seth Anderson
554 Beacon Road
Santa Barbara, CA 97770
805/555-2332

SANDRA L. PEARSON

12 E. Tenth Street
San Francisco, CA 98490
Home: 415-555-2343
Sandy.Pearson@xxx.com

January 30, 20--

Robert T. Beatty
Director of Personnel
Turner Broadcasting Co.
One Turner Plaza
Atlanta, GA 33203

Dear Mr. Beatty:

I am writing to you regarding the possibility of obtaining a position within your company in the area of advertising sales.

I have several years of sales experience, including work for Medialink Advertising Agency in San Francisco and KTUT-TV in Portland. As you can see from my resume, I have sold space for major clients in the automotive industry, advised on the content suitability of ads, and done demographic research.

I would like to utilize my sales experience in the growing cable television field. I believe that my extensive background would make for an easy transition into your company. I have enclosed my resume and look forward to hearing from you soon.

Sincerely,

Sandra L. Pearson

May 15, 20--

Deborah Klugh
Director of Human Resources
ABC
11 Rockefeller Plaza
New York, NY 10019

Dear Ms. Klugh:

This letter is in response to your ad in *The New York Times* for a P.R. assistant. I have enclosed my resume and salary requirements as requested.

Next month I graduate from Boston University with a degree in Communications and a concentration in Public Relations. I was inducted into Phi Beta Kappa this month and expect to graduate with honors.

I am interested in working in the television industry and would like to become part of the ABC team. I possess strong written and verbal communication skills and feel certain that I would do an excellent job in meeting the demands of this position.

Please feel free to contact me if you have any questions regarding my background. I am willing to travel to New York for an interview. Thank you for your time and consideration.

Sincerely,

Barton T. Quigley
Boston University
Fenton Hall
199 W. Hampshire Way
Boston, MA 02201
617/555-3839

Renee Glykison

8 E. Western Avenue • Houston, TX 75737 • 713/555-8098

January 14, 20--

Gekko Publishing, Inc.
1700 Avenue of Industry
Dallas, TX 78989
Attn: Ricardo Montoya, Director of Personnel

Dear Mr. Montoya:

This letter is a response to your advertisement in the *Houston Chronicle*'s classified section. The position of assistant manager of operations for a publisher of Gekko's stature is one that appeals to me greatly. I am enclosing my resume for your consideration in light of this opening.

Currently, I am assistant manager for a small but dynamic publisher in Houston: American National Books, Inc. My experience at American National includes orchestrating market analyses, identifying and meeting clients' needs, maintaining current accounts, and establishing new accounts. Previous to this position, I served as a sales representative for four years at Unico International in Dallas.

I am willing to come to Dallas for an interview at your convenience. Please feel free to contact me at either phone number listed below or via e-mail. I look forward to meeting you and discussing this opportunity.

Sincerely,

Renee Glykison

February 19, 20--

Q. T. Wollers
Tatum Advertising Agency
555 Paddington Avenue
Boston, MA 02214

Dear Ms. Wollers:

I am writing to inquire about openings in your agency for a graphic artist.
Currently, I manage the advertising department of the *New England
News*, where I conceive and design ads; oversee development, layout,
and typesetting; and maintain the financial records and accounts of the
department. While I find my current position quite challenging, my first
love and long-term goal is graphic design.

I have a solid educational background in the field of design, including
an M.A. in Graphic Design from the Cambridge School of Design and
a B.A. in Visual Communications from the University of Chicago.

I have enclosed my resume for your reference. I look forward to speaking with you about Tatum and the current openings in the agency. Thank
you for your time and consideration.

Sincerely,

Teresa Morbito
15 Fourth St. East
Boston, MA 02115
(602) 555-4009

W I N O N A   T .   S I M P S O N

420 W. Easterly Avenue   Home: 317/555-1267
Indianapolis, IN 49091   w.simpson@xxx.com

September 2, 20--

Thomas E. Eagletender
Pizza Hut, Inc.
4200 Bolt Ave.
Indianapolis, IN 48902

Dear Mr. Eagletender:

David Porter of your marketing department informed me that you were
looking for a new PR manager in the midwest office. Therefore, I have
enclosed my resume for your consideration.

Currently, I serve as PR director for Blockbuster Video in Indianapolis. Previous to Blockbuster, I worked as marketing representative for Jeron Stereo
and also as a public relations assistant for Kader Advertising.

My accomplishments include developing a successful marketing campaign for Blockbuster, implementing marketing strategies to increase sales
at less profitable outlets, and designing a training program for store managers and staff.

I believe my resume speaks for itself. I would very much like to meet with
you to discuss this position further. Please contact me at (317) 555-1267 at
your convenience.

Sincerely,

Winona T. Simpson

December 2, 20--

Corlis Fenett, Jr.
President
Venture Publishing Corp.
7 Rockefeller Plaza
New York, NY 10019

Dear Mr. Fenett:

As regional manager of *Coast Magazine*, I have faced many challenges and have handled each of them thoroughly, responsibly, and efficiently. In the past four years, I have learned and contributed a great deal to the magazine. In this position, I oversee administration, negotiation and maintenance of exchange agreements, and promotion. I have led the magazine's eastern edition through a difficult reorganization period and planned and implemented new editions in the south.

I have enjoyed my tenure at *Coast*, but I feel it is time to move on to a new challenge. This challenge, I hope, will be the position of Director of Operations at Venture Publishing Corp. Venture has a wonderful reputation as a progressive and challenging environment, and I believe my abilities would be an asset to your company.

I have enclosed my resume for your consideration. Please take a moment to review my skills and experience. I look forward to hearing from you and discussing this position further.

Sincerely,

Linda Carlisle

333 E. 20th St. #3
New York, NY 10019
212/555-2902

D A R R Y L   P A N D Y
3300 E. 17th St. #2
St. Louis, MO 54098
314/555-8979

September 9, 20--

Richard T. Yori
Director of Personnel
Sandler & Grey
333 N. Michigan Ave.
Chicago, IL 60601

Dear Mr. Yori:

I am writing to inquire about the copywriter opening with the Sandler & Grey Agency that was recently advertised in the *Chicago Tribune* classified section.

Currently, I work as an assistant copywriter for Porter & Cook in St. Louis, but I am looking to move to a position as copywriter. My experience includes writing copy for a newsletter and brochures, and specific product research. I feel that the experience I have gained in the last four years at Porter & Cook will qualify me for the position of copywriter. I graduated from Washington University Cum Laude with a B.A. in Advertising.

I have enclosed my resume for your consideration. I look forward to speaking with you soon.

Sincerely,

Darryl Pandy

October 17, 20--

David D. Geras
Director of Broadcast Operations
WGN-TV
700 W. Addison
Chicago, IL 60625

Dear Mr. Geras:

I enjoyed speaking with you at the Broadcast Careers seminar at Howard University last spring. I am writing to you to express my interest in an opening at WGN for a news assistant. I am enclosing my resume for your review.

Besides the B.A. degree in Journalism, which I will receive next month, I have gained experience over the last four summers in a variety of workplaces. Most recently, I completed an internship at WDC-TV in Washington, DC, where I assisted in the production of a news show. Previous internships include *Capitol Magazine*, *Chattanooga News*, and Park Advertising.

I would be glad to come to Chicago for an interview at your convenience. Thank you for your time and consideration.

Sincerely,

Terri Bakkemo
700 Thornborough Rd.
Chattanooga, TN 75221
615-555-2111

February 12, 20--

Wendell C. Wilkerson
Editor
Richmond Register
330 S. Potomac Drive
Richmond, VA 11980

Dear Mr. Wilkerson:

I am writing in response to your opening for a beat reporter, which was posted at the career office at the University of Virginia. I am currently seeking a position in the field of journalism and wish to be considered for this opening.

I graduated last June with a B.A. in Journalism from the University of Virginia with a GPA of 3.6. My writing and reporting experience includes two years as Senior Editor of the campus newspaper, editing of a literary magazine, and a broadcast journalism internship with WRCH-TV, all in Richmond.

My enclosed resume details my skills and experience. I believe that my background has prepared me for this challenge. I am available for an interview at your convenience. Thank you for your consideration.

Sincerely,

Trevor Haversmith
34 W. Greenview St. #3
Pennsylvania, PA 18978
804/555-3903

Rosemary Deborah Parker
5509 E. George Street, Apt. 442
Columbia, SC 29263
803-555-2893

November 19, 20--

Septimus J. Harper
Publisher
Time Magazine
1 Rockefeller Plaza
New York, NY 10019

Dear Mr. Harper:

I am writing to be considered for the position of editor for *Time* magazine.

I have spent the past seven years as assistant editor of *Carolina Woman*, where I have handled a variety of challenging tasks. During this time, I evaluated manuscripts, handled copyediting and rewriting, worked with artists and designers on layout aspects, and supervised the publication of a poetry anthology. Previous to my tenure at *Carolina Woman*, I also served as copyeditor for the *Raleigh Gazette*.

Time magazine would be a challenging and wonderful opportunity for me. I believe that I would be a great asset to your publication in the position of editor. Please contact me for an interview at your convenience.

Sincerely,

Rosemary Deborah Parker

Margaret Chapman

9484 N. Ellis Street   Home: 410/555-3949
Baltimore, MD 21203   Work: 410/555-5900 ext. 211

April 22, 20--

Mr. George Schonfeld
Senior Editor
Academic Press
Garden City, New York 11430

Dear Mr. Schonfeld:

Please accept the enclosed resume in response to your call for editors that appeared in the April issue of *Publishers Weekly*. I have ten years' experience as an editor and technical writer preparing publications and proposals for the scientific community.

My current position involves both production and acquisitions editing. It demands the same qualities you seek: strong organizational skills, the ability to work under pressure, and respect for deadlines.

I am familiar with your publication and admire the high editorial standard set for your books. It would be a pleasure to assist Academic Press as an employee.

Please let me know if you need any additional information to evaluate my credentials. I have enclosed my resume and three writing samples for your review. I look forward to hearing from you.

Sincerely,

Margaret Chapman

Notes

Notes

Notes

Notes

Notes